ON SOCIALISM

Additional Titles on Social and Political Philosophy in Prometheus's Great Books in Philosophy Series

Aristotle
The Politics

Mikhail Bakunin
The Basic Bakunin: Writings, 1869–1871

Edmund Burke
Reflections on the Revolution in France

John Dewey
Freedom and Culture

G. W. F. Hegel
The Philosophy of History

Thomas Hobbes
The Leviathan

Sidney Hook
Paradoxes of Freedom

Sidney Hook
Reason, Social Myths, and Democracy

John Locke
Second Treatise on Civil Government

Niccolo Machiavelli
The Prince

Karl Marx and Frederick Engels
The Economic and Philosophic Manuscripts of 1844 and
The Communist Manifesto

John Stuart Mill
Considerations on Representative Government

John Stuart Mill
On Liberty

John Stuart Mill
The Subjection of Women

Friedrich Nietzsche
Thus Spake Zarathustra

Thomas Paine
Rights of Man

Plato
Plato on Homosexuality: Lysis, Phaedrus, and *Symposium*

Plato
The Republic

Jean-Jacques Rousseau
The Social Contract

Mary Wollstonecraft
A Vindication of the Rights of Women

See the back of this volume for a complete list of titles in Prometheus's Great Books in Philosophy and Great Minds series.

ON SOCIALISM

JOHN STUART MILL

PROMETHEUS BOOKS • AMHERST, NEW YORK

Published 1987 by Prometheus Books
59 John Glenn Drive, Amherst, New York 14228-2197

Library of Congress Catalog Number: 87-61246
ISBN 0-87975-404-4

Printed in the United States of America on acid-free paper.

JOHN STUART MILL was born in London on May 20, 1806, the son of noted Scottish economist and philosopher James Mill, who held an influential post in the powerful East India Company. Mill's natural talent and physical stamina were put to the test at a very young age when he undertook a highly structured and individualized upbringing orchestrated by his father, who believed that the mind was a passive receptacle for human experience. His education and training were so intense that he was reading Greek at the age of three and doing independent writing at six.

Mill's education broadened considerably after 1823 when he entered the East India Company to commence his life's career as his father had done before him. He traveled, became politically involved, and, in so doing, moved away from the narrower sectarian attitudes in which he had been raised. His ideas and imagination were ignited by the views of such diverse personalities as Wordsworth, Saint-Simon, Coleridge, Comte, and de Tocqueville. During his life, Mill wrote many influential works: *System of Logic* (1843), *Principles of Political Economy* (1848), *On Liberty* (1859), *The Subjection of Women* (1861), *Utilitarianism* (1863), *Examination of Sir William Hamilton's Philosophy* (1865), and *Autobiography* (1873). As a defender of individual freedom and human rights, John Stuart Mill lives on as a nineteenth-century champion of social reform. He died on May 7, 1873. Mill's work on socialism was published posthumously in 1879.

Contents

Introduction

John Stuart Mill as a Sociologist: The Unwritten Ethology

Lewis S. Feuer

In 1843, at the height of his intellectual powers, and with his *System of Logic* published and recognized at once as an intellectual landmark, John Stuart Mill prepared for his next book.* Virtually announced at the end of his *Logic,* his aim now was to be to establish the foundations of sociology. Ethology, the science of "the laws of human character," was to have been the core; then he would set forth the laws both of social statics and dynamics. For a "considerable time"

Mill tried to write this book. But, as Alexander Bain, his friend, tells us, he "despaired, for the present time at least" of bringing such a work to fruition. Thereupon Mill turned in the autumn of 1845 to composing instead a volume on *Political Economy*.[1]

Among the great social thinkers of the nineteenth century, Mill was the only one who failed to write a system encompassing the evolution of humanity. Hegel, Comte, Marx, and Spencer felt they could enunciate and derive the law of social progress. Mill too would have wished greatly to prove that an empirical law of progress followed from the basic laws of mind. But Mill, author of "On the Logic of the Moral Sciences," the most enduring essay on the method of the social sciences which has ever been written, was aware that their simple "derivations" collapsed under scientific scrutiny.

Comte, Marx, and Spencer could enunciate laws of historical development because their perception was pre-selected by their categorical schemes; they saw a reality, censored through ideological prisms, which arbitrarily excluded a whole set of possible developmental sequences consistent with observable facts. Comte ruled out the likelihood that religious revivals might occur, a possibility which Tocqueville had documented, and he altogether vetoed the notion that anti-civilizational waves might reinstate astrology and fetishism in people's minds. Marx excluded the possible advent of technocratic, totalitarian societies, characterized by managerial rule rather than by the workers' self-administration. Spencer tended to set aside the possibility that the militant motive in men might manifest itself with a renewed intensity to engulf industrial societies; though in his later years he brooded over the possibility of a "re-barbarization," he never integrated his law of the differentiated progress of societies with his awareness of their possible decline. Mill alone tried to do justice to all the competing drives and motives of human nature; he would never banish from his consciousness the knowledge of the many-sidedness and many-levelledness of social reality. With his immense learning, practical experience, and logical acumen, Mill was more qualified to write the masterpiece of sociology than any other man in the nineteenth century. To understand why he failed in this design will perhaps bring to light truths of social existence that only great failures make explicit. What intellectual problems arose to make it impossible for Mill to compose his sociological treatise?

Mill in his *Logic* had explicated the character of the social sciences in a manner which has basically withstood all criticism. The inverse deductive method, as he called it, distinguished between the three levels of social analysis. Underlying all social truths there were first the elementary, fundamental laws of mind, the laws of psychology, known to us through introspection and empathic understanding. These provided the basic premises for sociology considered as a deductive science. The sociologist as a deductive theorist knew his major premises and indeed his empirical conclusions; he then sought the intervening minor premises which were still unknowns. The conclusions to be derived were the empirical laws of sociology, confirmed in statistical studies and surveys—such empirical laws, for instance, as those concerning the frequencies and variations of suicide which Quetelet was investigating in Mill's time.[2] Between the major premises of psychology and the empirical laws of sociology was the domain of the middle principles—the *axiomata media,* the laws of ethology. These were to constitute the science of the formation of national character, or social character as it would be called today. To every system or structure of social institutions, Mill affirmed, there was a corresponding formation of social character. The social institutions were the social initial conditions under which the universal laws of human psychology operated. And they gave rise to the laws of ethology, or social psychology—those forms of human feeling, thought, and behavior which social circumstances educed from the universal psychological nature of man. The observed empirical laws would then in turn be derivable from the laws of mind and the ethological premises.

Mill's conception of sociology is today part of its common sense. For instance, it provides the framework for the study of suicide, an example in which Mill was interested. Persons of Calvinist background usually show higher rates of suicide than Roman Catholics; again, for many years, the suicide rates among Negro men were about one-third those of white men in corresponding age groups. To explain these empirical uniformities of suicide, we would avail ourselves in Millite fashion of such psychological laws as we may possess. We might use the psychological law that where frustrations persist or increase, the aggressive energies accumulate; and that where the latter cannot be directed toward causative external objects, they are redirected inward against one's self. As sociologists, we should seek the ethological middle laws which would take us to the empirical uniformities. We might use the ethological law that the Calvinist upbringing made for a more rigorous, severe, unbending conscience, that its reproaches, moreover, were alleviated by no social servomechanism, and that the resultant guilt feelings were more intense. We might note that because the Negro family had for many years a matriarchal pattern, with the fathers of the children unknown or transient, the character-structure of the sons, therefore, was such in which the father's commands had a weaker part. And from these ethological laws we could derive the empirical uniformities of suicide.

As a model of what a science of ethology could do, Mill had before him his father's *History of British India,* a book which he had read in manuscript and which, as he said, guided his thoughts by its analysis of Hindu society and civilization; the son regarded it as perhaps the most instructive history ever written.[3] James Mill had traced the causes of the Hindu national character to their political institutions. His character-sketch of them was scarcely flattering: "No other race of men are perhaps so little friendly and beneficent to one another as the Hindus." Their "listless apathy" was not the outcome of their climate; other nations such as the Chinese had lived under as warm a sun but were "neither indolent, nor weak." If the Hindus disliked work, it was for one basic reason—their subjection to a wretched government, under which the fruits of their labor were never secure. Other Britons might find profundities in Hindu religious philosophy, but to James Mill their conception of nature was "the most grovelling and base" and their writings replete with "a more gross and disgusting picture of the universe" than any other people could adduce.[4]

There is a simplicity and comprehensiveness in John Stuart Mill's conception of sociology. It is utterly free of the exaggerations of later methodological schools which, fastening on one of Mill's three levels of analysis, have declared it to be the all-exclusive sociological one. Thus, Durkheim's school maintained that no psychological components should enter into a sociological explanation, though its own practice contravened its theory; on the other side, empirical surveyors have wished to pursue their inquiries without regard to underlying causal laws; while phenomenologists have argued that only the inner psychological processes, bracketed from the external world, were the social reality. Mill stood above such academic ideologies.

It was the very comprehensiveness of Mill's inverse deductive method, however, that made it impossible for him to bind together the contrary empirical laws he wished to affirm. To begin with, there was the flat contradiction in Mill between the manifest nineteenth-century optimist and the underlying pessimist. As an optimist, he accepted Auguste Comte's law of the three stages—the evolution from the religious to the metaphysical to the positive stage—as a valid empirical generalization; Comte's "main conclusions," he wrote, were sound, and the chain of causation Comte outlined was "in all essentials irrefragable"; this intellectual movement, Mill said further, was "at the root of all the great changes in human affairs."[5] But then there was the pessimist Mill who discerned that the law of the future would be the dominance of mediocrity: "the general tendency of things throughout the world is to render mediocrity the ascendant power among mankind." "[I]n the world at large," wrote Mill, there was "an increasing inclination to stretch unduly the powers of society over the individual. . . ." It was the sociological analogue to the great generalization which William Thomson, later Lord Kelvin, had enunciated at almost the same time on the universal tendency to the dissipation of energy. In not dissimilar words, Mill affirmed: "the tendency of all the changes taking place in the world is to strengthen society, and diminish the power of the individual. . . ." The creative energies of men would become increasingly unavailable.

Most unfortunately, according to Mill, no social class or stratum was exempt from the tendency toward mediocrity. The middle classes, the masses, and the reforming intellectuals were all alike mediocrats and intolerant. In England, said Mill, it was "chiefly the middle class" which imposed the stamp of its "collective mediocrity" on social existence;[6] in democratic America, it was the "whole white population" expressing itself through the force of public opinion;[7] and as for the intellectuals, "almost all the projects of social reformers of these days are really *liberticide.*"[8] From Saint-Simon to August Comte, their aim had been "dictatorship," and with Comte it seemed indeed that the crypto-despot in every revolutionizing intellectual emerged explicit: in his scheme for "the absolute and undivided control of a single Pontiff for the whole human race—one is appalled at the picture of entire subjugation and slavery. . . ."[9]

Here then were two empirical laws which stood as contraries to each other—progress and mediocritization. The contraries in his ethological laws also tore apart the psychological basis which Mill provided for his sociology. In his *Logic,* following in his father's footsteps, Mill asserted that the laws of association were a sufficient foundation for the explanation and derivation of sociological laws. Yet, it became clear to Mill, a far broader conception of human drives was required. He noted in his essay "Nature" (begun in 1854) that there was "an instinct for domination" in men, "a delight in exercising despotism, in holding other beings in subjection to our will"; it was linked to an "instinct for destructiveness," "an instinct to destroy for destruction's sake"; men were "naturally cruel."[10] Comte too had observed that there were two "very powerful instincts," "a downright taste for destruction" and a repugnance toward labor, which impelled men toward military rather than industrial societies.[11] If so, however, civilization rested on a precarious "victory over instinct" through self-discipline. There were "bad instincts" in men which, said Mill, "it should be the aim of education not simply to regulate, but to extirpate. . . ."[12] But if so, on what psychological ground could an empirical law of progress safely repose? The laws of mind, as Mill set them forth, were consistent not only with mediocritization, but indeed with a decline of civilization. What combination of psychological axioms with middle principles would underwrite the empirical law of progress?

Now Karl Marx, confronted by essentially the same problem, could avail himself of the salvaging motor force of the dialectic. According to Marx and Engels, greed and the lust for power could themselves be enlisted to transform a system beset with "contradictions" into a higher one. But this conception was explicitly repudiated by Mill, most clearly so in his essay on Guizot's theory of history. Guizot, Marx's forerunner as a historian of class struggles, had affirmed that feudal society, "by its own nature and tendencies," evolved toward its dissolution. Mill, however, saw no such dialectic transmutation of evil to a higher good. "That is an easy solution," he wrote, "which accounts for the destruction of institutions from their own defects; but experience proves that forms of government and social arrangements do not fall merely because they deserve to fall. The more backward and the more degraded any form of society is, the stronger is the tendency to remain stagnating in that state, simply because it is an existing state."[13] Existing societies, far from being "rational" or "functional," were, from Mill's standpoint, as likely or likelier to be irrational and otiose. Then, how then did the feudal society evolve into a free commercial and industrial one? Progress, according to Mill, took place not because of any dialectical breakdown, but rather because the spirit of liberty, the aspiration toward improvement, had found within the feudal order a sufficient support. Given the "imputed causes of the fall of feudalism, the question recurs," wrote Mill, "what caused the causes themselves? . . . There can be but one answer; the feudal system with all its deficiencies, was sufficiently a government, contained within itself a sufficient mixture of authority and liberty . . . to enable the natural causes of social improvement to resume their course." The feudal age, in Mill's view, had been wrongly "vilified," for "at no period of history was human intellect more active, or society more unmistakably in a state of rapid advance" than during a great part of it.

Only once did Mill in an ethical fervor allow himself to endorse the notion that an evil institution must perish of economic necessity. That was during the American Civil War when Mill argued in 1862 that the confinement of slavery to the Southern states would mean its "death-warrant," its "nearly inevitable and probably rapid" extinction.[14]

Underlying all progressive change, in Mill's view, was simply a persisting moral aspiration in men which could never be stifled but rather endured through all the "compressions" of human character to avail itself of the rare social circumstances which enabled humanity to resume its linear advance. "All political revolutions, not effected by foreign conquest, originate in moral revolutions," wrote Mill.[15] Revolutions of progress were in his view the consequence of an uprising of the spirit of liberty and improvement against the "yoke of authority." Mill thus attributed the rise of capitalist society, or in his terms, the rise of "the principle of accumulation," to conditions which allowed "the growth of mental activity, making the people alive to new objects of desire." Under such conditions of a better government and more complete security, foreign arts were welcomed; "by instilling new ideas and breaking the chains of habit, if not by improving the actual condition of the population, [it] tends to create in them new wants, increased ambition, and greater thought for the future."[16] If Mill was ranged against any Marxist dialectical conception, he would also have rejected the involuted dialectic of Max Weber wherein Calvinist asceticism somehow gave rise to its precise opposite, the development of new industries and new wants. According to Mill, Calvinism constituted a "narrow theory of life" making for a "pinched and hidebound type of human character," for people "cramped and dwarfed," crushing the individual and his will through self-denial, and refusing to conceive of God as a Being who takes delight in every increase of human "capabilities of comprehension, of action, or of enjoyment."[17] As such, it would be inimical to the free development of the sciences and technology essential to the rise of capitalism. Calvinist doctrine too easily afforded a justification for what Mill called "an equal chance to everybody of tyrannizing," a desire, he said, as "fully natural to mankind" as the desire not to be tyrannized over.[18]

Nonetheless, a sociological mystery still persisted as to

the circumstances in which the spirit of liberty and advancement would prevail over the drives toward enslavement and retrogression.

Mill at one point tried to found the empirical law of progress on two universal human motives—the pursuit of truth and "the desire of increased material comforts." The latter, the hedonistic ingredient, was, he wrote, "the impelling force" to most improvements. But, he went on to observe, the "progress of industry must follow, and depend on, the progress of knowledge."[19] Every advance in material civilization has been preceded, wrote Mill, by an advance of knowledge; changes in the mode of thought, in the Comtist pattern, have set the stage for these advances, but these changes in the mode of thought have themselves not arisen from the requirements of practical life but solely from the inner tendency of the previous system of beliefs to evolve. Once again, however, Mill's sociological theory was in straits. For what immanent law prescribed that a system of beliefs had to evolve? If it was dominated by myths, why could not a society stagnate in the mythological mode even as it did in its economy? What gave power to the pursuit of truth so that it could triumph over the contrary will to illusion?

At this juncture Mill tended to shift the causal primacy in social evolution to the character of a people's political institutions. He asserted in his *Logic* as a basic principle "the necessary correlation between the forms of government existing in any society and the contemporaneous state of civilization. . . ."[20] The greatness of the Athenian achievement, he thus affirmed, was derived from their free social institutions.[21] By contrast, the impoverished backwardness of many fertile tracts of Asia received its "acknowledged explanation" in the tyrannical insecurity of rapacious governments, whose agents could deprive one arbitrarily of the fruits of one's labor. Why did the Roman empire decline? Mill felt that Finlay had explained this phenomenon better than had Gibbon,[22] for Finlay traced the decrease in the Italian population to evils inherent in the political system of the Roman government, its public distribution of grain, its arbitrary mode of taxation.[23] But the relation between social institutions and a people's mode of thought and feelings was also asserted by Mill to be circular, interdependent, and interactive, with neither variable ontologically independent: "The creed and laws of a people act powerfully upon their economic conditions; and this again by its influence on their mental development and social relations reacts upon their creed and laws."[24]

Mill, however, could scarcely be satisfied with a theory of the multiple causal interdependence of social institutions and modes of thought. It was adequate for what he (following Comte) called static rather than dynamic situations. Thus an equilibrium was defined by the uniformities between a society's different elements of coexistence; the society's institutions would all be values to interdependent mathematical functions, and the static state of affairs would be the counterpart of mathematical conditions of equilibrium. Yet these static mutual correlations themselves arose out of dynamic processes; they were the terminal points of equilibrium of processes in which one variable might well indeed be the primary independent. The aspiration for liberty, truth, and improvement seemed never to be confined to particular static forms consistent with their coexistent society; the dynamic variables always had a degree of freedom which resisted their simply being assigned the values appropriate to the existing institutions.

Mill at this point verges on a complete declaration for sociological voluntarism as against sociological determinism. For years he had struggled with the problem of determinism. It weighed on him not only logically, but psychologically, part of that "nightmare" which (in Thomas Henry Huxley's expression) haunted British thinkers of that era. During the "mental crisis" of his early manhood, it took the form, as Mill described it, of his being "seriously tormented by the thought of the exhaustibility of musical combination." He compared "this source of anxiety" to "that of the philosophers of Laputa, who feared lest the sun should be burnt out." Then in "later returns of my dejection," as Mill wrote, "the doctrine of what is called Philosophical Necessity weighed on my existence like an incubus. I felt as if I was scientifically proved to be the helpless slave of antecedent circumstances. . . ."[25] He struggled to remove this incubus all his life. He drew the distinction in later years between two kinds of fatalism, the Asiatic and the modified, which he contrasted with his own doctrine. "Real Fatalism is of two kinds. Pure, or Asiatic fatalism—the fatalism of the Oedipus—holds that our actions do not depend upon our desires." In the case of modified fatalism, "our actions are determined by our will," wrote Mill, "our will by our desires," and the last are determined by our motives and character; our character, however, is supposed to have "been made for us and not by us, we are not responsible for it. . . ." The true doctrine of causation, on the contrary, said Mill, affirmed that our character is "in part amenable to our will. . . ." Yet it scarcely seemed that Mill had escaped the fatalism of the Oedipus.

All the varieties of fatalism and his own causation as well reduced to an Oedipal determinism. For our decisions and efforts to improve our characters were all in principle predictable; the behavior of Mill and the modified fatalist were as predictable as that of the Oedipal subject in whose case a superior power intervened as an added variable. This common predictability pervaded all of Mill's thought with something akin to an Oedipal determinism.[26] His sociological theory tried to make real the power of mankind to choose and be unbound by universal laws. But he could never define a sense of freedom which would liberate him from Philosophical Necessitarianism. Perhaps his choice of the Oedipal metaphor to convey the sense of the extreme of fatalism reveals something of the emotional source of the hold of determinism upon Mill.

It was in his *Political Economy* above all that Mill explicated what he thought was the scientific basis for social choice; he drew the distinction between the laws of production with their necessitarian character and the laws of distribution which were voluntarist. Mankind, rescued from sociological fatalism, was acknowledged to be able to choose the kind of society it wanted:

> The laws and conditions of the production of wealth, partake of the character of physical truths. There is nothing optional or arbitrary in them. . . .
>
> It is not so with the Distribution of Wealth. That is a matter of human institution solely. The things once there, mankind, individually or collectively, can do with them as they like. . . . The rules by which it is determined, are what the opinions and feelings of the ruling portion of the community make them, and are very different in different ages and countries; and might be still more different, if mankind so chose.[27]

Thus, the law of diminishing returns was, according to Mill, essentially a law of chemistry and physics stated with reference to agricultural technology; the laws of distribution, on the other hand, bore the stamp of man's varying choices. Mill drew on his own experience and knowledge of Indian affairs to illustrate how human choices could be made among diverse possible social systems. The British authorities had introduced different social systems in India; sometimes they displaced an oligarchy of usurpers and collected the taxes directly; in other cases they decided to create landed aristocracies; and in still others they cooperated with the representatives of village communities to arrest social change. Thus, human choice had been efficacious in deciding among the alternatives to the existent system of land ownership.[28]

If choices were genuine, mankind might then choose to progress rather than retrogress or stagnate. The incubus of sociological necessitarianism would be lifted. Yet, choice remained a kind of surd in Mill's sociological theory. For a sociology of choices always was at hand in his own terms to subsume them under causal laws. Mill strongly rejected the doctrine, akin to the Marxian, that "the forces . . . on which the greater political phenomena depend, are not amenable to the direction of politicians or philosophers." According to this doctrine of sociological necessitarianism, "the government of a country, it is affirmed, is in all substantial respects, fixed and determined beforehand by the state of a country in regard to the distribution of the elements of social power."[29] Choice, according to such a doctrine, was the experience of a social epiphenomenon; the deliberations of philosophers never liberated the so-called choices from their determinants of social power. "Whatever is the strongest power in society will obtain the governing authority. . . . A nation, therefore, cannot choose its form of government." And James Mill had long previously analyzed the situation of a country divided into a ruling class and a subject class as one in which the members of the former had sympathies almost exclusively for themselves.

To this doctrine of economic determinism, Mill replied that purely ethical convictions, contravening the material interests of economic and social power did intervene at critical junctures to transcend the latter: "It was not by any changes in the distribution of material interest, but by the spread of moral convictions that negro slavery has been put an end to in the British Empire and elsewhere." The emancipation of the Russian serfs was, he felt, another decision which transcended material interests. Then wrote Mill: "It is what men think, that determines how they act. . . ."[30] Even on his own showing, however, it was very rare that men's thoughts contravened their economic interests. For as he affirmed in *On Liberty:* "Wherever there is an ascendant class, a large portion of the morality of the country emanates from its class interests. . . ."[31]

And, indeed, was that segment of men's ideas which transcended material interests free from causal determination? Were acts which transcended selfishness likewise choices in the sense of transcending causal laws? There were moments in the world's history, as in the February Revolution of 1848 in France, when it seemed to Mill that there appeared "that almost unheard-of-phenomenon—unselfish politicians"; decisions then seemed to become choices rather than the resultants of polygons of social forces.[32] One might argue that the causal processes of individual psychology would account for these materially transcending actions. But there was no causal account at hand to explain how these idealistic motives, so powerless ordinarily, could have persisted in human history to shape its outlines and demarcate its future development. The instinct of domination was so much more forceful; hatred, selfishness, and brutality were so omnipresent that one asked: How had this puny vector of aspiration to truth and fellow-feeling survived in this welter of barbarian forces? That civilization had risen as far as it had against the evil inscribed in man's animal nature seemed a cosmo-historical fact of such improbable proportions that its actual occurrence defied the categories of sociological understanding. Thus it was that Mill was driven toward a sociological theology.

Mill's last essay, on theism, "dismayed his disciples," wrote John Morley. It was a natural conclusion, however, to his lifetime of sociological reflections. Mill had survived troughs of despair, such times as when he found human beings so abhorrent that he speculated with a certain pleasure upon the conditions under which there might take place a "universal & simultaneous suicide of the whole human race."[33] He had reflected on how beautiful the English environment would be but for its people: "The nuisance of England is the English."[34] Nonetheless, this human race seemed somehow to have surmounted partially and periodically the trammels of its heredity and circumstances. Man had fashioned for himself, wrote Mill, "a second nature, far better and more unselfish than he was created with."[35] The virtues—courage, cleanliness, truth-telling—were all conquests of instinct; man evolved not through conforming to nature, but from his resolve to amend it, to challenge the maleficient powers. Whence, however, did he derive the resolve to challenge his own given character and status in animal existence? There was the feeling, Mill wrote, that in such an effort "we may be cooperating with the unseen Being to whom we owe all that is enjoyable in life." This God was a Limited God, not omnipotent. To his closest disciples Mill seemed suddenly and inexplicably to have subscribed to a Manichaean theology. Yet Mill found himself drawn to such postulates by processes of thought not dissimilar to those which have moved such scientists as Einstein, Bohr, Heisenberg, Russell. Einstein discerned the counterpart of Spinoza's Substance in the all-embracing simple laws of nature; Niels Bohr was moved in his conception of physical quanta by a vision of Kierkegaardian stages; Heisenberg and Max Born sought to realize conceptions of free will; while Russell hoped that a Kropotkinite anarchism prevailed at least among the world of logical atoms. In a similar sense, Mill found himself affirming a metasociological postulate: "a battle is constantly going on, in which the humblest human creature is not incapable of taking some part, between the powers of good and those of evil, and in which every even the smallest help to the right side has its value in promoting the very slow and often almost insensible progress by which good is gradually gaining ground from evil. . . ." This postulate in Mill's view was "the most animating and invigorating thought which can inspire a human creature," and he allowed that it might be grounded in a hope which reached toward the supernatural.[36]

Thus Mill at the close of the utilitarian cycle moved toward views which his father James Mill had put aside seventy-five years earlier. John Stuart Mill regarded himself as "one of the very few examples, in this country, of one who has not thrown off religious belief, but never had it. . . ."[37] The father had "after many struggles" painfully shed his Presbyterian creed, and affirmed that "concerning the origin of things nothing whatever can be known." He had, however, kept open for consideration "the Manichaean theory of a Good and an Evil Principle, struggling against each other for the government of the universe. . . ."[38] And the son now felt that such an inarticulate premise was adumbrated in his experience; the sociologist's inverse deductive method, the laws of mind, and the empirical sociological laws, required the intervening metasociological principle of a Limited God.

Mill's sociological Manichaeanism, moreover, was not a sudden aberration of old age. He had used its vocabulary and metaphors spontaneously at the outset of the American Civil War when he had pleaded that England should not for the sake of cotton render aid to the Confederacy and make "Satan victorious"; the Southern secessionists, he wrote, were undertaking "to do the devil's work."[39] And, indeed, a Manichaean world view has been a largely unspoken axiom of sociologists; only Mill had the courage to articulate it. Physicists such as Einstein might find in the conception of God a regulative principle leading to the discovery of simple, mathematical laws. Is this the way God would have done it? was the question Einstein always asked. Not so, however, with social reality. The sociologist asks as well: How would social reality have been contrived if Satan had had his share in designing it? If God provides a methodological regulative criterion in physical science, Satan provides a partial one in social science. Malthus seeing disaster latent in every happiness of man, Marx and Engels writing of history as a goddess demanding human sacrifices, Weber describing a rationalization of life which made people ever more disenchanted, Pareto seeing idealists pursuing illusions in an endless circulation of élites, all shared a common standpoint with Mill who brooded in 1848 that "it is questionable if all the mechanical inventions yet made have lightened the days' toil of any human being."[40]

Indeed, Mill's Manichaeanism led him to enunciate what was perhaps his most original sociological theorem—his theory of the stationary state. The evolution of society, according to Mill, has an upper limit: "It must always have been seen, more or less distinctly, by political economists, that the increase of wealth is not boundless: that at the end of what they term the progressive state lies the stationary state, that all progress in wealth is but a postponement of this, and that each step in advance is an approach to it. We have now been led to recognize that this ultimate goal is at all times near enough to be fully in view. . . ." Gone was Condorcet's vision of the indefinite progress of man. His was a law of sociological impotence (to use the term of the physicist Edmund Whittaker): "This impossibility of ultimately avoiding the stationary state—this irresistible necessity that the stream of human industry should finally spread itself out into an apparently stagnant sea. . . ."[41] In essence, Mill derived this theorem from the simple consideration that the practice and development of the industrial arts always involved the depletion of energy resources. The stationary state was a corollary of the second law of thermodynamics applied to the closed system of the planet Earth. But where other economists and sociologists such as Marx paid homage to the everlasting development of the forces of production and industrial civilization, and would have regarded the stationary state as too remote to enter the sociological purview, Mill avowed himself frankly as not charmed by "the trampling, crushing, elbowing, and treading on each other's heels, which form the existing type of social life."[42] He wanted solitude and the preservation of natural beauty. To Marx who wrote of "the idiocy of rural life" he counterposed the imbecility of urban life, and he spent his most joyous days in botanizing, in long tramps, which led to "frequent notes and short papers" in *The Phytologist,* an obscure journal for botanical collectors.[43] The Limited God of Mill had his counterpart in the finitude of energy resources. If the human species must finally vanish, its one hope was at least to postpone that not distant event by the wise cultivation of a stationary state, stationary in capital, population, and the productive arts.[44]

Is Mill's theory of the stationary state a viable one? Mill felt that in the stationary state "there would be as much scope as ever for all kinds of mental culture"; the art of living, the arts and sciences would indeed, he argued, improve even more "when minds ceased to be engrossed by the art of getting on."[45] What Mill failed to pursue, however, were the social consequences of a stationary state. For such a society would probably evoke the most intense generational conflicts; bereft of the sense of open frontiers and opportunities, the young would expend their energies of aggression and hatred even more unidirectionally upon the old. In prehistoric stationary societies, the middle-aged men evidently died by violence.[46] The Chinese stationary society, which Mill studied, was characterized by a severe discipline imposed on the young; the sciences and arts of living were virtually transfixed. A stationary society would be one without the experience of renaissances. The condition for healthy social existence is that it be revivified for the young with the breath of fresh new industries and material obstacles; otherwise aggressive energies might turn inward, toward self-destruction.

Moreover, every wave of human improvement has been founded on a contemporaneous expansion of capital. It is sociologically doubtful that the arts of life could progress without such a corresponding material progress. And with the depletion of energy resources, a society would be unable to maintain its stationary position without progress in the use of its industrial capital and available resources.

The author of *On Liberty* feared slackening and stagnation; the theorist of the stationary state, however, regarded it as the best compromise with Manichaean reality that the human race might hope to achieve. Here was still another reason why Mill was unable to write his sociology. Not the contradictions of Victorian England were laid bare in his thought but rather the eternal unresolvable oppositions within all human life.

Some might say that Mill's theory of the stationary state was a reflection of the death-instinct which periodically waxed strongly in him.[47] To which Mill could reply that he alone in the nineteenth century had not flinched from drawing the ultimate consequences of Thomas Malthus's mode of thought.[48] And perhaps the Limited God, if not himself possessed of a death-instinct, was finally incapable of sustaining the human race against the harsh odds of the material universe.

Withal, it is probably true that Mill's sociological pessimism, his pervasive sense of pending exhaustion, had its highly personal sources as well. His up-bringing by his father had so constrained him that he wrote poignantly: "Let any man call to mind what he himself felt on emerging from boyhood. . . . Was it not like the physical effect of taking off a heavy weight. . . ? Did he not feel twice as much alive. . . ?"[49] Above all, the strains of the two decades of his sexual repression with respect to Harriet Taylor had exacted their toll. To mitigate these strains, Mill cultivated a mocking attitude not unlike Harriet's toward those who made much of the strength of the sexual drive. He railed at those who said it was difficult to control the sexual appetite.[50] He declared that the possibility of progress itself depended on the reduction of sexuality, that no great improvement in human life could be looked for "so long as the animal instinct of sex occupies the absurdly disproportionate place it does therein"; and he anticipated confidently that this passion would become "with men, as it is already with a large number of women, completely under the control of reason"—that is, as disciplined as he was in emulation of Harriet.[51] He persuaded the historian George Grote to delete from the Preface to his *History* the words "feminine" and "masculine" in the discussion of the aspects of the ancient Greek character. He showed an unusual sympathy toward the medieval institution of a celibate clergy.[52] Mill's *Autobiography* impressed Freud as "so prudish or so ethereal that one could never gather from it that human beings consist of men and women, and that this distinction is the most significant one that exists."[53]

Yet, periodically, resentment against the régime of sexual attenuation would break forth. He had ridiculed as a young man the search of the Saint-Simonians for "la femme libre," which had indeed sent them to a quest among the harems of Constantinople. But in his old age, his final tribute to the Saint-Simonians was to "the boldness and freedom from prejudice with which they treated the subject of the family, the most important of any, and needing more fundamental alterations than remain to be made in any other great social institution, but on which scarcely any reformer has the courage to touch."[54] He responded with dislike to the statue of the Venus de Medici, saying "the expression of the face is complete old maidism."[55] Above all, in his unconscious he argued, though not very successfully, with Harriet's high discipline. He wrote her an account of a memorable dream: "I was seated at a table like a table d'hôte, with a woman at my left hand & a young man opposite—the young man said, quoting somebody for the saying, 'there are two excellent & rare things to find in a woman, a sincere friend and a sincere Magdalen.' I answered 'the best would be to find both in one'—on which the woman said 'no, that would be *too* vain—whereupon I broke out 'do you suppose when one speaks of what is good in itself, one must be thinking of one's own paltry self-interest? no, I spoke of what is abstractedly good and admirable.'"[56] Mill finally recognized explicitly that his father James together with his fellow Associationists obliterated sexuality and the biological basis of emotions from psychology. James Mill had dismissed the whole subject delicately with one sentence: "The affection of the husband and wife is, in its origin, that of two persons of different sex, and need not be further analyzed."[57] By contrast, John wrote: "there is evidently in all our emotions an animal part . . . which these philosophers have passed without any attempt at explanation."[58] The phenomenon of "intense bodily suffering," the "screams, groans, contortions, etc.," the experience and manifestations of Fear, were systematically omitted by the Associationist.

Mill's own experience, borne too stoically, had left him imprinted with a permanent dislike for human society. One wonders finally whether Mill at the last would have interceded with any enthusiasm with his Limited God to spare the human race. He could scarcely engage in the kind of panoramic mythologizing and ideologizing to which Karl Marx could surrender himself; he lacked Marx's capacity to disregard doubts, and to rely on dialectical paste-paper to bridge the transitions between the stages of society as well as collapsing arguments.

There are signs that the father James Mill felt at times a restiveness with his own life and was rebellious toward the austere Calvinist asceticism which still underlay his Benthamite associations of pleasure. He was strangely drawn to the personality of the South American revolutionary general, Francisco de Miranda. As the French Saint-Simonians later fed the exotic longings of his son, so General Miranda delighted the Calvinist calculating utilitarian with his effervescence and spontaneity. The general was famed for exploits which had likened him to Casanova; the lover of the admired Delphine de Custine, who had escaped the guillotine which annihilated her family, he had been characterized by the Emperor Napoleon as "a Don Quixote except that he is quite sane." Under Miranda's influence, James Mill felt himself fortified to reject his traditional religion. James worked together with the general on an article "Emancipation of Spanish America," published in 1809 in the *Edinburgh Review*. He rendered tribute to the general as one in whose "breast the scheme of emancipation, if not first conceived, seems at least to have been first matured."[59] Betrayed in the revolutionary war, Miranda died in 1816 in a Spanish dungeon. Meanwhile, James Mill had found in vicarious revolutionary participation an alleviation of the strains of a grey doctrine, a harsh Presbyterian upbringing, and an unhappy marriage. The son John repeated the pattern. The misfortune of James Mill's life was that he too had known a Harriet Taylor, but in his case their separation was inevitable. She was the daughter of the Scottish baron, Sir John Stuart, after whom James had named his son. James wrote about her as his son did of Harriet: "besides being a beautiful woman, [she] was in point of intellect and disposition one of the most perfect human beings I have ever known." They grew up and studied together from childhood on, "and were about the best friends that either of us ever had." When she was dying, she spoke of James "with almost her last breath."[60] James Mill could never forget that his wife was not the one he loved. His utilitarianism was as much the outcome of a personal quarrel with society as his son's *On Liberty*.

Mill did try periodically to alleviate the pessimistic tendencies in his character and his sociological theory by partaking in the enthusiasm and fellowship of socialist movements. Nevertheless, in the final consideration, he always refrained from any overt commitment to socialism, and at the time of his death was writing what even in its fragmentary form was the most powerful critique of socialism written in the nineteenth century. As a young man, Mill had long, eager discussions with the young French Saint-Simonian Jew, Gustave d'Eichthal, whom he admired almost as much as his father had venerated the Dutch-English Jew David

Ricardo. He shared the revolutionary zeal of the Saint-Simonians, and almost became one of them; tactical considerations alone, he said, kept him from enlistment in their ranks. Meanwhile, he awaited the revolutionary hurricane:

> And if the hour were yet come for England . . . I know not that I should not renounce everything and become, not one of you, but as you.
>
> But our 10 août, our 20 juin, and perhaps our 18 Brumaire, are yet to come. And which of us will be left standing when the hurricane has blown over, Heaven only knows.[61]

This period of high revolutionary zeal was also that of his growing involvement with Mrs. Harriet Taylor, the period of his most intense rebellion against the authority of his father James Mill. He wrote in 1831 to his close friend Sterling with the swathes of the revolutionary intellectual: "until the whole of the existing institutions of society are levelled with the ground, there will be nothing for a wise man to do. . . ." And he looked forward with pleasure to what later would be called the "physical liquidation" of the English middle class and its intellectual advocates. It will be recalled that the father James was an unashamed admirer of the middle class.[62] The son, however, wrote that if only "a few dozens of persons" were salvaged to be "missionaries of the great truths" for posterity, he would "not care though a revolution were to exterminate every person in Great Britain and Ireland who has £500 a year. Many very amiable persons would perish, but what is the world the better for such amiable persons?"[63] Mill's ideological, Messianic mood coincided with his peaks of aggressive resentment. But with his awesome strength of character, he always regained his rationality and independence of judgment. He finally estimated the Saint-Simonians as having a "narrow & bigoted understanding, & a sordid & contracted disposition," and being so fixated on the notion that history was governed by a unidirectional progressive law that they forgot it could go backwards.[64] He welcomed the advent of the International Workingmen's Association in 1864 when Karl Marx, to please the British labor leaders, allowed himself to write like a Millite rather than a Marxist. But when the secretary of its Nottingham branch sent Mill its literature, he responded that, though he "warmly approved" of its principles: "What advantage is there in designating the doctrines of the Association by such a title as 'the principles of the political and social Revolution?'"[65] Mill in his *Autobiography* classed himself and Harriet "under the general designation of Socialists." During the subsequent years, however, he kept himself well-informed through reading the journals of the Association.[66] His misgivings concerning socialism deepened. He had always been troubled by what he saw as "the social problem of the future"—how to preserve "the greatest individual liberty" within the framework of a socialist society.[67] He now however observed those whom he called "the revolutionary socialists," and concluded that the motives which impelled them were malevolent. Those "who play this game," he wrote, "unconfirmed as yet by any experimental verification . . . and [who] would brave the frightful bloodshed . . . must have a serene confidence in their own wisdom on the one hand and a recklessness of other people's sufferings on the other, which Robespierre and St. Just, hitherto the typical instances—scarcely came up to." For Mill stated clearly what he took to be the tenets of the "revolutionary socialists"; they were exactly those of Marx. They proposed on the economic side, wrote Mill, "the management of the whole productive resources of the country by one central authority," while on the political side "their purpose" was "that the working classes, or somebody in their behalf, should take possession of all the property of the country, and administer it for the general benefit." Thus, the three elements of the revolutionary socialist programme were total central planning, the alleged ownership of the national property by the working class, and its achievement by a revolutionary act. Their avowed aim was "to substitute the new rule for the old at a single stroke, and to exchange the amount of good realized under the present system, and its large possibilities of improvement, for a plunge without any preparation into the most extreme form." The programme had "great elements of popularity," Mill noted, not shared by "the more cautious and reasonable form of Socialism." For it made its appeal above all to the emotions of hatred. This, then, was the ethological middle principle of revolutionary socialism: "for if appearances can be trusted, the animating principle of too many of the revolutionary Socialists is hate." One might undertake to excuse their absorption in hatred by evoking their dialectical belief, in Mill's words, "that out of chaos would arise a better Kosmos." But this entirely overlooked, wrote Mill, "that chaos is the very most unfavorable position for setting out in the construction of a Kosmos, and that many ages of conflict, violence, and tyrannical oppression of the weak by the strong must intervene. . . ." In the character of the dialectical revolutionists Mill perceived a readiness to destroy the world if it could not be changed: "its apostles could have only the consolation that the order of society as it exists now would have perished first, and all who benefit by it would be involved in the common ruin. . . ."[68]

The leaders of the English workingmen alone, Mill observed with some pride, refused to be drawn into the destructivism of the European revolutionary socialists. "The leaders of the English working-men—whose delegates at the congresses of Geneva and Bâle contributed much the greatest part of such practical common sense as was shown there—are not likely to begin deliberately by anarchy. . . ."[69] The congresses of the International Workingmen's Association in September 1866 and 1869 had been the scene of a struggle between Marx's faction and the followers of Proudhon. Marx's initial programme for the International, adopted at Geneva, was rather moderate, placing the emphasis on achieving the eight-hour day and a system of public education; it stressed, however, the importance of trade unions as agencies for "complete emancipation" whereas the Proudhonists advocated cooperative associations and denigrated the recourse to strikes. At Basel, however, the legendary figure of Mikhail Bakunin emerged to lead the most formidable challenge to Marx's "centralized Communism" on behalf of anarchy; Bakunin indeed won majorities against Marx in the actual voting on resolutions. The English trade-union leaders supported Marx's proposals as against Bakuninist anarchy, yet they too were unhappy with the underlying note of Marx's "centralized Communism." Mill stood with such trade unionists as Odger, Cremer, and Applegarth, against both Marx and Bakunin; the English trade unionists soon dissociated themselves from the International. Marx at the last Congress of the International in 1872 insulted all the English labor leaders by saying publicly that "almost every recognized leader of the English working men was sold to Gladstone, Morley, Dilke and others."[70] The English laborites never forgave him for that slur. The enfranchisement of 1867 had opened up to the British working class the prospect of using Parliament to achieve social reforms; thus seeds which were being planted for the Labor party were far more Millite than Marxist.[71] Mill's last chapters on socialism must be regarded as essentially an evaluation founded on the added experience of the English trade unionists with the International. He knew that they had been at odds with all the ideologists, with Marx, Bakunin, and Proudhon. The too generous hopes of Mill in 1848 for the principle of association were now basically amended in the light of this new phenomenon of the revolutionary ideologists—this permeation of socialism with a ferocity and hatred which Mill had not previously foreseen.

No doubt Karl Marx was informed through their various common associates, the labor leaders and the positivist intellectuals, of Mill's opinion of "revolutionary socialists." Nothing else would explain Marx's outburst against John Stuart Mill in the closing days of the International, on 16 April 1872, months after Mill had protested the sanguinary suppression of the Paris Communards.[72] Mill still continued to place some hope in a moderate, experimental, piecemeal socialism which could "be brought into operation progressively, and . . . prove its capabilities by trial." With sympathy toward communitarians (exemplified in later years by Martin Buber and William Morris), Mill looked to modest efforts "on the scale of a village community." Aware, no doubt, that experiment had often shown that such associations deteriorated into village tyrannies, Mill as a pluralist noted the aim for "the multiplication of such self-acting units."[73] Perhaps individual liberty might be safeguarded in a society of competing communal associations. Yet, in 1849 Mill had affirmed his belief that cooperative associations would not prove themselves as efficient as competitive societies.[74]

The notion of central planning itself, "the very idea of conducting the whole industry of a country by direction from a single center," was in Mill's view "obviously chimerical."[75] "Communistic management" would be "less favorable than private management to that striking out of new paths"; it would lack the venturesomeness "generally indispensable to great improvements in the economic condition of mankind. . . ."[76] It would of necessity decide "in a more or less arbitrary manner" those questions which "on the present system" for all its imperfections decide themselves spontaneously—that is, in predominant accord with rational criteria.[77] Thus in a few sentences Mill raised those problems concerning the irrationality of socialist economy which have haunted the halls of socialist proponents of later generations, and whose phantom still attends the sessions of the Soviet Planning Council. Curiously, the corollary latent in Mill's analysis was that for a communist society taken in isolation the optimal equilibrium would be that of a stationary state. Mill indeed had written Harriet Taylor in 1849 that the objection to communism that it would make life "a kind of dead level" could never be taken away.[78] Nevertheless, he always clung to elements of a socialist ethic even though his analysis dissociated socialist society from any law of progress with which it had been joined so facilely by socialists.

Meanwhile, however, Mill finally rejected the notion that the misery of the working classes was increasing under capitalism. This was one of the "Socialist exaggerations," he wrote. "The present system is not, as many Socialists believe, hurrying us into a state of general indigence and slavery from which only Socialism can save us. The evils and injustices suffered under the present system are great, but they are not increasing; on the contrary, the general tendency is towards their slow diminution."[79] He still looked for guidance to the moral principles of socialism, but doubted whether in the trials of experiment the power of the "higher" motives would be sufficient even in a large minority to sustain such a society.[80] It had become clear to Mill that for the revolutionary socialists the experience of the revolutionary leap and the opportunities it afforded for the release of aggression was the primary purpose; they disliked an experimental approach toward socialist ventures precisely because it deprived them of the chance for revolutionary experience. In 1849 Mill had charged that the fear of socialism drove the bourgeoisie into an "insane terror."[81] At the end of his life he might have amended this statement to make central instead the fear not so much of socialism as of socialists, such as Blanqui, whose aim was the savoring of revolutionary dictatorship far more than the improvement of the human lot. What the sources of this compulsion for revolutionary experience might be was a problem that was left unsolved for a more developed science of ethology.

Mill was, it must be remembered, part of that corps of British sociologists whose ideas were largely shaped by their experience in the administration of India. Though Mill's work was confined to the London headquarters of the East India Company, he was dealing with the same problems that Sir Henry Maine and James Fitzjames Stephen met in India directly.[82] The administrative experience provided Mill's judgment with a ballast which Marx and Comte never had. He knew the inefficiencies and arbitrariness in the bureaucratic administration in a way the bookmen-revolutionists never did. With respect to problems where he lacked that ballast, Mill too tended to veer toward radical proposals otherwise foreign to him. He, for instance, like his friend John Cairnes, demanded in Abolitionist fashion that all Negro ex-slaves be given the right to vote at the end of the American Civil War. He would have repudiated such a demand for the people of India whom he regarded as still in their "nonage." In the former case, he was moved by pure ethics; in the latter, he weighted ethics with sociological experience. Ethical zeal, at times, could obliterate Mill's social judgment. For instance, he finally opposed the secret ballot because he felt that all men should be fearless in character, and not afraid to say openly what they thought. But the Cooperative leader, George Jacob Holyoake, thought that Mill had forgotten that a secret ballot gave the average man his only chance to be independent—that Mill expected the average citizen to have the character of a John Stuart Mill.[83]

What then is Mill's place in the development of sociological science? His enduring greatness is as the conscience of science. Virtually alone he sought steadfastly to keep his sociology free from ideology. He articulated the problems which others repressed by a variety of devices. Where Marx and Engels projected a dialectical leap which would take human society from the kingdom of necessity to that of freedom, Mill, too honest to succumb to the allure of sociological metaphor, enquired into the threats which socialism would pose for individual liberty. While Weber built a whole theory of the origins of capitalism on a presumed psychological law that guilt-ridden people will embark more frequently upon technological innovation, Mill, with his analysis of the Calvinist character, would scarcely acquiesce to such an assumed law of mind. Where Durkheim as a Radical Republican exalted society and claimed that religion was society's worship of itself, Mill would observe that religious ideals provided a basis for the critique of every existing society; if religion was society's self-worship, then the tension between religion and society was unintelligible. Mill could never write a complete system of sociology because he alone would not confuse the subjective completeness of a narrowed mind with the objective completeness of sociological explanation.

That is why when we look for intellectual guidance today with respect to the problems of freedom in communist societies, the exhaustion of the environment, and the pressure of population, Mill is the only sociologist of the nineteenth century whose pages are not discolored with the acid of bias. Others claiming to prefigure the law of history, were obsessed by the demon of making history; Mill held to the more modest ethic of acting as circumstances allowed on behalf of human happiness. In so doing, the "saint of rationalism" held to the conception of scientific truth with an integrity which the prophet-ideologists never approached.

NOTES

*This essay was originally read by the author at the Centenary Conference for James and John Stuart Mill at the University of Toronto on May 3-5, 1973, and printed in *James and John Stuart Mill: Papers of the Centenary Conference,* edited by John M. Robson and Michael Laine (University of Toronto Press, 1976). Copyright reserved to the author, Toronto, 1976.

1. Alexander Bain, *John Stuart Mill: A Criticism With Personal Recollections* (London 1882), 78-79, 84.

2. Quetelet, it should be observed, created the science of social statistics during the early 1830s when he and the young Belgian intellectuals were, like young Mill in England, under the influence of Saint-Simonian ideas. See Lambert A. J. Quetelet, *A Treatise on Man and the Development of his Faculties,* facsimile of 1842 translation, introduction by Solomon Diamond (Gainesville 1969), vi, vii. In making psychological laws the basis for those of sociology, Mill opposed Comte's view that a science of psychology was impossible.

3. *Autobiography,* ed. J. Stillinger (Boston 1969), 16-17.

4. *The History of British India,* 5th ed. (1858; reprinted New York, 1968), I, 466, 469, 480, 481, 371, 385, 347.

5. *August Comte and Positivism,* in John Stuart Mill, *Collected Works,* X (Toronto 1963-82), 317, 319, 322-23. *Collected Works* will hereafter be abbreviated as CW.

6. *On Liberty,* 4th ed. (London 1869), 119.

7. Ibid., 118-19.

8. Letter to Harriet Mill, 15 Jan. 1855, CW, XIV, 294.

9. *Considerations on Representative Government,* 3rd ed. (London 1865), 38-40; *August Comte and Positivism,* CW, X, 351.

10. "Nature," CW, X, 398.

11. Auguste Comte, *System of Positive Polity,* tr. E. S. Beesly et al. (London 1875-77), III, 47.

12. CW, X, 393, 398.

13. "Guizot's Essays and Lectures on History," *Dissertations and Discussions: Political, Philosophical, and Historical,* II (London 1859), 268-70.

14. J. S. Mill, "The Contest in America," *Dissertations and Discussions,* III (London 1867), 191.

15. J. S. Mill, "A Few Observations on the French Revolution," *Dissertations and Discussions,* I (London 1859), 56.

16. *Principles of Political Economy,* CW, II, 186-87.

17. *On Liberty,* 112.

18. *Principles,* CW, III, 944.

19. *Logic,* CW, VIII, 926 (VI, X, 7).

20. CW, VIII, 919 (VI, X, 5).

21. *Dissertations and Discussions,* II, 286.

22. John Morley, *Recollections* (London 1917), I, 66.

23. "The social organization of nations affects their vitality as much as their political constitution affects their power and fortunes." George Finlay, *A History of*

Greece, from its conquest by the Romans to the present time, B.C. 146 to A.D. 1864, new ed. (Oxford 1877), I, 89-90.

24. *Principles,* CW, II, 3.

25. *Autobiography,* 87, 101.

26. Freud in 1880 translated a volume of Mill which included his essays on the labor question, Harriet Taylor Mill's "The Enfranchisement of Women," Grote's *Plato,* and the posthumous writings on socialism. He did so at the request of Mill's Viennese friend and editor, Theodore Gomperz. Did Freud read the other translated volumes, and imbibe Mill's usage of the "fatalism of the Oedipus"? In any case, Freud regarded Mill "as perhaps the man of the century who best managed to free himself from the domination of customary prejudices." (Ernest Jones, *The Life and Work of Sigmund Freud* [New York 1953], 1, 55, 176). Apart from the essays on socialism, the contents of the volume Freud translated were drawn from Volume II of *Dissertations and Discussions.* Mill's views on the hatred-vector in revolutionary socialism clearly became the basis for Freud's analysis of communism. Compare Adelaide Weinberg, *Theodor Gomperz and John Stuart Mill* (Geneva 1963) 60.

27. *Principles,* CW, II, 199-200.

28. "Mr. Maine on Village Communities," *Fortnightly Review,* ns, IX, 1871, 554-5.

29. *Representative Government,* 12. The action of the British people in abolishing the slave trade and in emancipating the slaves was, Mill wrote, "a cause in which we not only had no interest, but which was contrary to our pecuniary interest. . . ." *(Dissertations and Discussions,* III, 180).

30. J. S. Mill, *Representative Government,* 15. James Mill, *Analysis of the Phenomena of the Human Mind,* 2nd ed. (London 1869), II, 275n.

31. *On Liberty,* 16.

32. "Vindication of the French Revolution of February 1848," *Dissertations and Discussions,* II, 337.

33. Letter to Harriet Mill, 30 Dec. 1854, CW, XIV, 272. John Morley, op. cit., p. 106.

34. Letter to Harriet Mill, 2 Jan. 1855, CW, XIV, 277.

35. "Theism," CW, X, 459.

36. Ibid., 488-89.

37. *Autobiography,* 27-8. Bain, however, writes that "John as a little boy, went to church; his maiden aunt remembered taking him, and hearing him say in his enthusiastic way 'that the two greatest books were Homer and the Bible.' " *(James Mill,* 90).

38. *Autobiography,* 25-26.

39. "The Contest in America," *Dissertations and Discussions,* III, 181.

40. *Principles,* CW, III, 756.

41. Ibid., 752.

42. Ibid., 754.

43. Henry Trimen, "His Botanical Studies," H. Fox Bourne, ed., *John Stuart Mill — His Life and Works* (Boston 1873), 44. Mill's botanizing was throughout his life the avocation in which he found the most complete pleasure. He first became a plant-collector during his sojourn in Southern France, 1820-1, "the happiest six months of my youth." He would pursue it intensely day after day in arduous climbs and hikes whenever he could. When the "battle of the Barricades" was raging in 1832 during the crisis of the Reform bill, Mill was off botanizing quietly at Highgate. He told Herbert Spencer his "murderous propensities" were "confined to the vegetable world." (Anna Jean Mill, ed., *John Mill's Boyhood Visit to France* [Toronto 1960], 65).

44. *Principles,* CW, III, 752-57.

45. Ibid., 756.

46. See Carlo M. Cipolla, *The Economic History of World Population,* rev. ed. (Middlesex 1964), 74.

47. Leslie Stephen felt that Mill's theory of the stationary state was rather a temporary protest than a settled conviction. *(The English Utilitarians* [London 1900], III, 200).

48. When young Oliver Wendell Holmes, Jr., visited Mill in 1866, Mill took him to a meeting of the Political Economy Club where the subject for discussion was "whether the financial policy of England should be governed by the prospective exhaustion of coal in H years as predicted by Jevons . . ." (Mark De Wolfe Howe, *Justice Oliver Wendell Holmes: The Shaping Years* [Cambridge, Mass. 1957], 226-27).

49. *The Subjection of Women* (London 1869), 180-81.

50. Bain, *John Stuart Mill,* 149.

51. Letter to Lord Amberley, 2 Feb. 1870, CW, XVII, 1693; Diary entry, 26 March, in Hugh Elliot, *Letters of John Stuart Mill* (London 1910), II, 382.

52. Bain, *John Stuart Mill,* 78, 86. J. S. Mill, "Michelet's History of France," *Dissertations and Discussions,* II, 159.

53. Ernest Jones, *The Life and Work of Sigmund Freud* (New York 1953), I, 176.

54. Letter to Carlyle, 11 & 12 April 1833, CW, XII, 150; *Autobiography,* 101.

55. Letter to Harriet Mill, 8 June 1855, CW, XIV, 480.

56. Letter to Harriet Mill, 17 Feb. 1857, CW, XV, 523-24; *John Stuart Mill and Harriet Taylor,* 254.

57. James Mill, *Analysis,* II, 218-19.

58. "Bain's Psychology," *Dissertations and Discussions,* III, 132-33.

59. Bain, *James Mill,* 89. William Spence Robertson, *The Life of Miranda*

(Chapel Hill 1929), II, 48-50; I, 57. Joseph F. Thorning, *Miranda: World Citizen* (Gainesville 1952), 126. George F. Kennan, *The Marquis de Custine and his Russia in 1839* (Princeton 1971), 3-4.

60. Graham Wallas, *The Life of Francis Place: 1771-1854* (4th ed., London 1925), 70-1.

61. Letter to Gustave d'Eichthal, 30 Nov. 1831, CW, XII, 89.

62. Letter to John Sterling, 20-22 Oct. 1831, CW, XII, 78. The "class which is universally described as both the most wise and the most virtuous part of the community, the middle rank . . . which gives to science, to art, and to legislation itself their most distinguished ornaments . . ." (James Mill, *An Essay on Government* [reprinted, Cambridge 1937], 72-2).

63. Letter to Sterling, 20-2 Oct. 1831, CW, XII, 84.

64. Letter to Gustave d'Eichthal, 8 Oct. 1829, CW, XII, 37.

65. Edward S. Mason, *The Paris Commune: An Episode in the History of the Socialist Movement* (New York 1930), 50.

66. Letter to Georg Brandes, 4 March 1872, CW, XVII, 1874-75. A subscription on Mill's behalf to the journal *Progress* was made by Cowell Stepney, an eccentric blind millionaire who was a member of the International's General Council. (See James Guillaume, *L'Internationale: Documents et Souvenirs* [Paris 1905], I, 1939.)

67. *Autobiography,* 138.

68. *On Socialism,* this ed. 115-17, 135-36.

69. *On Socialism,* this ed. 61. George Odger, the secretary of the London Trades Council, supported Mill increasingly while he denounced the intransigence of the General Council of the International, "the most unfit persons I have ever come in contact with to represent the working classes." George Howell, who in 1871 became secretary to the Parliamentary committee of the Trades Union Congress, advised workers to "get Mill on Liberty and Political Economy. There are many other works, but go to the fountain head at once." Marx fought Mill's influence in the labor movement by supporting the Land and Labor League against Mill's Land Tenure Reform Association. Mill in turn deplored "the furious and declamatory virtue" of the former's resolutions. (See Royden Harrison, *Before the Socialists: Studies in Labor and Politics, 1861-1881* [London 1965], 234, 143, 223).

Mill always exerted his logical powers to dissuade the English labor leaders from being captivated by revolutionary rhetoric and violent postures. In March 1867 he wrote to William Randal Cremer in sharp disapproval of the calls for force which the Reform League was making to secure enactment of the bill for enfranchisement. Ultimate success in Britain, Mill said, could only be obtained "by a succession of steps." No justification for "revolutionary expedients" existed in the British case (CW, XVI, 1247-48). He argued in September 1865 with George Howell, who placed an inordinate faith in the strike weapon; where strikes were successful in the generality of trades, said Mill, there would be a general rise in prices, which would be of "no benefit to the laboring classes" (CW, XVI, 1102). But he subscribed in 1869 to the Labor Representation League on whose executive Howell was active (CW, XVII, 1673). He vigorously supported Odger in his efforts to win election to Parliament: "No one has taken a warmer interest than I have in the candidatures of working men in general & Mr. Odger in particular, & I believe Mr. O. is well aware of this," Mill wrote in 1870 (ibid., 1688). And when Odger lost again in February 1870 Mill still wrote him a letter of congratulation (ibid., 1697). He wrote in terms of admiration of the English labor leaders, and in December 1867 advised Thomas Hare, the exponent of proportional representation: "if you could make a convert of even one such man as Odger, or Cremer, or Howell — the gain would be immense" (CW, XVI, 1342). He introduced to Odger his "very old friend," the former Saint-Simonian, Gustave d'Eichthal, when the latter was visiting Britain in May 1871 (CW, XVII, 1816). It was Odger who rose to commend Mill at the celebrated meeting when Mill, a candidate for Parliament, acknowledged that he had written that the English working class were "generally liars." When the "vehement applause" subsided, Odger said that the working class "wanted friends, not flatterers," and were grateful to one who spoke sincerely of their faults (Mill, *Autobiography,* 168). To John Hales, the secretary of the General Council of the International, Mill wrote on 28 May 1871 saying that if any demonstration "could arrest or mitigate the horrors now being perpetrated at Paris" there was hardly anything he would not do; but he saw no such hope (CW, XVII, 1821-22). He gave his support to preventing the dismissal from University College of Professor E. S. Beesly, the courageous Comtist professor of classics who in 1867 had spoken in defense of the trade unions (CW, XVI, 1297).

70. Henry Collins and Chimen Abramsky, *Karl Marx and the British Labor Movement: Years of the First International* (London 1965), 260. Socialists and trade unionists generally admired the record of John Stuart Mill as a member of Parliament. William Morris said Mill had been "a real success in Parliament." (See James Mavor, *My Windows on the Street of the World* [London 1922], I, 209.) J. George Eccarius, Marx's collaborator on the General Council, wrote: "As a member of Parliament Mill conducted himself in exemplary fashion, and showed he had the courage to come forward in the interest of the working class to oppose both the aristocracy as well as the money-following bourgeoisie. His political behavior is in contradiction with his economic philosophy." *(Eines Arbeiters Widerlegung der National-ökonomischen Lehren John Stuart Mill's* [Berlin 1869], iv). On the reaction of the British labor leaders to Marx's insult, see Boris Nicolaievsky and Otto Maenchen-Helfen, *Karl Marx: Man and Fighter,* tr. Gwenda David and Eric Mosbacher (Philadelphia 1936), 360. John Hales moved a vote of censure against Marx in the British Federal Council; it was adopted. An amendment charging Marx with

political deception got an equally divided vote. (See Franz Mehring, *Karl Marx: The Story of His Life,* tr. Edward Fitzgerald [New York 1935], 518.)

71. "The economic influence most potent among the Socialist radicals is still that of John Stuart Mill." Sidney Webb, *Socialism in England,* 2nd. ed., (London 1893), 185.

72. Marx ridiculed what he called "John Stuart Mill's compendium of political economy," and the proposal, for instance, that the state should lend capital to co-operative societies, a proposal made by Ferdinand Lassalle and in keeping with Mill's idea. *(The General Council of the First International, 1871-1872: Minutes* [Moscow nd], 160) Marx's ire was especially directed against Henry Fawcett, professor of Political Economy at Cambridge, and Mill's disciple. Fawcett, after studying the documents of the International and after "frequent conversations with many of its members," gave a series of lectures in 1872 against its principles. Though himself, like Mill, an advocate of cooperation on the Rochdale model, Fawcett argued that the effort to realize the programme of the International would make for a "weakening and lessening of individual responsibility" and a decline of the "industrial virtues." (Henry Fawcett, "The Nationalization of the Land," *Fortnightly Review,* ns LXXII [1872], 627, 637, 638. Leslie Stephen, *Life of Henry Fawcett,* 5th ed. [London 1886], 158-66, 470).

73. *On Socialism,* this ed. 115.

74. "The French Revolution of 1848 and its Assailants," *Dissertations and Discussions,* II, 394.

75. *On Socialism,* this ed. 134.

76. Ibid., 123-24.

77. Ibid., 127.

78. Letter to Harriet Taylor, 21 Feb. 1849, CW, XIV, 11. Mill's concern for Harriet Taylor's approbation led him to mute his criticism of communism. In revising his *Political Economy* in 1849 he had stated the objections to communism that he thought were valid, but he wrote in conciliatory fashion: "if you do not think so, I certainly will not print it." (Ibid.) Mill argued with her that she "greatly" overrated "the ease of making people unselfish," and that even if they had absolute power, "all our plans would fail from the impossibility of finding fit instruments" (21 March 1849, ibid., 19). This passage in my opinion is not given sufficient weight by H. O. Pappé in his *John Stuart Mill and the Harriet Taylor Myth* (Melbourne 1960), 40. Not until Harriet was long dead was Mill able to bring all his critical acumen to bear on the socialist proposals.

79. *On Socialism,* this ed. 112.

80. Ibid., 113, 119-24.

81. *Dissertations and Discussions,* II, 394.

82. For twenty-three years Mill wrote almost every "political" dispatch of the

East India Company; two huge volumes, five or six inches thick, were each year written by Mill alone. (See W. T. Thornton, "His Career in the India House," *John Stuart Mill,* ed. Fox Bourne [Boston 1873], 32.)

83. George Jacob Holyoake, *Bygones Worth Remembering* (London 1905), I, 276.

On Socialism

Preliminary Notice

It was in the year 1869 that, impressed with the degree in which, even during the last twenty years, when the world seemed so wholly occupied with other matters, the socialist ideas of speculative thinkers had spread among the workers in every civilized country, Mr. Mill formed the design of writing a book on Socialism. Convinced that the inevitable tendencies of modern society must be to bring the questions involved in it always more and more to the front, he thought it of great practical consequence that they should be thoroughly and impartially considered, and the lines pointed out by which the best speculatively-tested theories might, without prolongation of suffering on the one hand, or unnecessary disturbance on the other, be applied to the existing order of things. He therefore planned a work which should go exhaustively through the whole subject, point by point; and the four chapters now printed are the first rough drafts thrown down towards the foundation of that work. These chapters might not, when the work came to be competely written out and then re-written, according to the author's habit, have appeared in the present order; they might have been incorporated into different parts of the work. It has not been without hesitation that I have yielded to the urgent wish of the editor of this Review to give these chapters to the world; but I have complied with his request because, while they appear to me to possess great intrinsic value as well as special application to the problems now forcing themselves on public attention, they will not, I believe, detract even from the mere literary reputation of their author, but will rather form an example of the patient labor with which good work is done.

HELEN TAYLOR

January, 1879

One

Introductory

In the great country beyond the Atlantic, which is now well-nigh the most powerful country in the world, and will soon be indisputably so, manhood suffrage prevails. Such is also the political qualification of France since 1848, and has become that of the German Confederation, though not of all the several states composing it. In Great Britain the suffrage is not yet so widely extended, but the last Reform Act admitted within what is called the pale of the Constitution so large a body of those who live on weekly wages, that as soon and as often as these shall choose to act together as a class, and exert for any common object the whole of the electoral power which our present institutions give them, they will exercise, though not a complete ascendancy, a very great influence on legislation. Now these are the very class which, in the vocabulary of the higher ranks, are said to have no stake in the country. Of course they have in reality the greatest stake, since their daily bread depends on its prosperity. But they are not engaged (we may call it bribed) by any peculiar interest of their own, to the support of property as it is, least of all to the support of inequalities of property. So far as their power reaches, or may hereafter reach, the laws of property have to depend for support upon considerations of a public nature, upon the estimate made of their conduciveness to the general welfare, and not upon motives of a mere personal character operating on the minds of those who have control over the Government.

It seems to me that the greatness of this change is as yet by no means completely realized, either by those who opposed, or by those who effected our last constitutional reform. To say the truth, the perceptions of Englishmen are of late somewhat blunted as to the tendencies of political changes. They have seen so many changes made, from which, while only in prospect, vast expectations were entertained, both of evil and of good, while the results of either kind that actually followed seemed far short of what had been predicted, that they have come to feel as if it were the nature of political changes not to fulfill expectation, and have fallen into a habit of half-unconscious belief that such changes, when they take place without a violent revolution, do not much or permanently disturb in practice the course of things habitual to the country. This, however, is but a superficial view either of the past or of the future. The various reforms of the last two generations have been at least as fruitful in important consequences as was foretold. The predictions were often erroneous as to the suddenness of the effects, and sometimes even as to the kind of effect. We laugh at the vain expectations of those who thought that Catholic emancipation would tranquilize Ireland, or reconcile it to British rule. At the end of the first ten years of the Reform Act of 1832, few continued to think either that it would remove every important practical grievance, or that it had opened the door to universal suffrage. But five-and-twenty years more of its operation have given scope for a large development of its indirect working, which is much more momentous than the direct. Sudden effects in history are generally superficial. Causes which go deep down into the roots of future events produce the most serious parts of their effect only slowly, and have, therefore, time to become a part of the familiar order of things before general attention is called to the changes they are producing; since, when the changes do become evident, they are often not seen, by cursory observers, to be in any peculiar manner connected with the cause. The remoter consequences of a new political fact are seldom understood when they occur, except when they have been appreciated beforehand.

This timely appreciation is particularly easy in respect to the tendencies of the change made in our institutions by the Reform Act of 1867. The great increase of electoral power which the Act places within the reach of the working classes is permanent. The circumstances which have caused them, thus far, to make a very limited use of that power, are essentially temporary. It is known even to the most inobservant, that the working classes have, and are likely to have, political objects which concern them as working classes, and on which they believe, rightly or wrongly, that the interests and opinions of the other powerful classes are opposed to theirs. However much their pursuit of these objects may be for the present retarded by want of electoral organization, by dissensions among themselves, or by their not having reduced as yet their wishes into a sufficiently definite practical shape, it is as certain as anything in politics can be, that they will before long find the means of making their collective electoral power effectively instrumental to the promotion of their collective objects. And when they do so, it will not be in the disorderly and ineffective way which belongs to a people not habituated to the use of legal and constitutional machinery, nor will it be by the impulse of a mere instinct of levelling. The instruments will be the press, public meetings and associations, and the return to Parliament of the greatest possible number of persons pledged to the political aims of the working classes. The political aims will themselves be determined by definite political doctrines; for politics are now scientifically studied from the point of view of the working classes, and opinions conceived in the special interest of those classes are organized into systems and creeds which lay claim to a place on the platform of political philosophy, by the same right as the systems elaborated by previous thinkers. It is of the utmost importance that all reflecting persons should take into early consideration what these popular political creeds are likely to be, and that every single article of them should be brought under the fullest light of investigation and discussion, so that, if possible, when the time shall be ripe, whatever is right in them may be adopted, and what is wrong rejected by general consent, and that instead of a hostile conflict, physical or only moral, between the old and the new, the best parts of both may be combined in a renovated social fabric. At the ordinary pace of those great social changes which are not effected by physical violence, we have before us an interval of about a generation, on the due employment of which it depends whether the accommodation of social institutions to the altered state of human society, shall be the work of wise foresight, or of a conflict of opposite prejudices. The future of mankind will be gravely imperilled, if great questions are left to be fought over between ignorant change and ignorant opposition to change.

And the discussion that is now required is one that must go down to the very first principles of existing society. The fundamental doctrines which were assumed as incontestable by former generations, are now put again on their trial. Until the present age, the institution of property in the shape in which it has been handed down from the past, had not, except by a few speculative writers, been brought seriously into question, because the conflicts of the past have always been conflicts between classes, both of which had a stake in the existing constitution of property. It will not be possible to go on longer in this manner. When the discussion includes classes who have next to no property of their own, and are only interested in the institution so far as it is a public benefit, they will not allow anything to be taken for granted—certainly not the principle of private property, the legitimacy and utility of which are denied by many of the reasoners who look out from the standpoint of the working classes. Those classes will certainly demand that the subject, in all its parts, shall be reconsidered from the foundation; that all proposals for doing without the institution, and all modes of modifying it which have the appearance of being favorable to the interest of the working classes, shall receive the fullest consideration and discussion before it is decided that the subject must remain as it is. As far as this country is concerned, the dispositions of the working classes have as yet manifested themselves hostile only to certain outlying portions of the proprietary system. Many of them desire to withdraw questions of wages from the freedom of contract, which is one of the ordinary attributions of private property. The more aspiring of them deny that land is a proper subject for private appropriation, and have commenced an agitation for its resumption by the State. With this is combined, in the speeches of some of the agitators, a denunciation of what they term usury, but without any definition of what they mean by the name; and the cry does not seem to be of home origin, but to have been caught up from the intercourse which has recently commenced through the Labor Congresses and the International Society, with the continental Socialists who object to all interest on money, and deny the legitimacy of deriving an income in any form from property apart from labor. This doctrine does not as yet show signs of being widely prevalent in Great Britain, but the soil is well prepared to receive the seeds of this description which are widely scattered from those foreign countries where large, general theories, and schemes of vast promise, instead of inspiring distrust, are essential to the popularity of a cause. It is in France, Germany, and Switzerland that anti-property doctrines in the widest sense have drawn large bodies of working men to rally round them. In these countries nearly all those who aim at reforming society in the interest of the working classes profess themselves Socialists, a designation under which schemes of very diverse character are comprehended and confounded, but which implies at least a remodelling generally approaching to abolition of the institution of private property. And it would probably be found that even in England the more prominent and active leaders of the working classes are usually in their private creed Socialists of one order or another, though being, like most English politicians, better aware than their Continental brethren that great and permanent changes in the fundamental ideas of mankind are not to be accomplished by a *coup de main,* they direct their practical efforts towards ends which seem within easier reach, and are content to hold back all extreme theories until there has been experience of the operation of the same principles on a partial scale. While such continues to be the character of the English working classes, as it is of Englishmen in general, they are not likely to rush headlong into the reckless extremities of some of the foreign Socialists, who, even in sober Switzerland, proclaim themselves content to begin by simple subversion, leaving the subsequent reconstruction to take care of itself; and by subversion they mean not only the annihilation of all government, but getting all property of all kinds out of the hands of the possessors to be used for the general benefit; but in what mode it will, they say, be time enough afterwards to decide.

The avowal of this doctrine by a public newspaper, the organ of an association *(La Solidarité,* published at Neuchâtel), is one of the most curious signs of the times. The leaders of the English working men—whose delegates at the congresses of Geneva and Bâle contributed much the greatest part of such practical common sense as was shown there—are not likely to begin deliberately by anarchy, without having formed any opinion as to what form of society should be established in the room of the old. But it is evident that whatever they do propose can only be properly judged, and the grounds of the judgment made convincing to the general mind, on the basis of a previous survey of the two rival theories, that of private property and that of Socialism, one or other of which must necessarily furnish most of the premises in the discussion. Before, therefore, we can usefully discuss this class of questions in detail, it will be advisable to examine from their foundations the general questions raised by Socialism. And this examination should be made without any hostile prejudice. However irrefutable the arguments in favor of the laws of property may appear to those to whom they have the double prestige of immemorial custom and of personal interest, nothing is more natural than that a working man who has begun to speculate on politics, should regard them in a very different light. Having, after long struggles, attained in some countries, and nearly attained in others, the point at which for them, at least, there is no further progress to make in the department of purely political rights, is it possible that the less fortunate classes among the "adult males" should not ask themselves whether progress ought to stop there? Notwithstanding all that has been done, and all that seems likely to be done, in the extension of franchises, a few are born to great riches, and the many to penury, made only more grating by contrast. No longer enslaved or made dependent by force of law, the great majority are so by force of poverty; they are still chained to a place, to an occupation, and to conformity with the will of an employer, and debarred by the accident of birth both from the enjoyments, and from the mental and moral advantages, which others inherit without exertion and independently of desert. That this is an evil equal to almost any of those against which mankind have hitherto struggled, the poor are not wrong in believing. Is it a necessary evil? They are told so by those who do not feel it—by those who have gained the prizes in the lottery of life. But it was also said that slavery, that despotism, that all the privileges of oligarchy were necessary. All the successive steps that have been made by the poorer classes, partly won from the better feelings of the powerful, partly extorted from their fears, and partly bought with money, or attained in exchange for support given to one section of the powerful in its quarrels with another, had the strongest prejudices opposed to them beforehand; but their acquisition was a sign of power gained by the subordinate classes, a means to those classes of acquiring more; it consequently drew to those classes a certain share of the respect accorded to power, and produced a corresponding modification in the creed of society respecting them; whatever advantages they succeeded in acquiring came to be considered their due, while, of those which they had not yet attained, they continued to be deemed unworthy. The classes, therefore, which the system of society makes subordinate, have little reason to put faith in any of the maxims which the same system of society may have established as principles. Considering that the opinions of mankind have been found so wonderfully flexible, have always tended to consecrate existing facts, and to declare what did not yet exist, either pernicious or impracticable, what assurance have those classes that the distinction of rich and poor is grounded on a more imperative necessity than those other ancient and long-established facts, which, having been abolished, are now condemned even by those who formerly profited by them? This cannot be taken on the word of an interested party. The working classes are entitled to claim that the whole field of social institutions should be reexamined, and every question considered as if it now arose for the first time; with the idea constantly in view that the persons who are to be convinced are not those who owe their ease and importance to the present system, but persons who have no other interest in the matter than abstract justice and the general good of the community. It should be the object to acertain what institutions of property would be established by an unprejudiced legislator, absolutely impartial between the possessors of property and the nonpossessors; and to defend and justify them by the reasons which would really influence such a legislator, and not by such as have the appearance of being got up to make out a case for what already exists. Such rights or privileges of property as will not stand this test will, sooner or later, have to be given up. An impartial hearing ought, moreover, to be given to all objections against property itself. All evils and inconveniences attaching to the institution in its best form ought to be frankly admitted, and the best remedies or palliatives applied which human intelligence is able to devise. And all plans proposed by social reformers, under whatever name designated, for the purpose of attaining the benefits aimed at by the institution of property without its inconveniences, should be examined with the same candor, not prejudged as absurd or impracticable.

Two

Socialist Objections to the Present Order of Society

As in all proposals for change there are two elements to be considered—that which is to be changed, and that which it is to be changed to—so in Socialism considered generally, and in each of its varieties taken separately, there are two parts to be distinguished, the one negative and critical, the other constructive. There is, first, the judgment of Socialism on existing institutions and practices and on their results; and secondly, the various plans which it has propounded for doing better. In the former all the different schools of Socialism are at one. They agree almost to identity in the faults which they find with the economical order of existing society. Up to a certain point also they entertain the same general conception of the remedy to be provided for those faults; but in the details, notwithstanding this general agreement, there is a wide disparity. It will be both natural and convenient, in attempting an estimate of their doctrines, to begin with the negative portion which is common to them all, and to postpone all mention of their differences until we arrive at that second part of their undertaking, in which alone they seriously differ.

This first part of our task is by no means difficult; since it consists only in an enumeration of existing evils. Of these there is no scarcity, and most of them are by no means obscure or mysterious. Many of them are the veriest commonplaces of moralists, though the roots even of these lie deeper than moralists usually attempt to penetrate. So various are they that the only difficulty is to make any approach to an exhaustive catalogue. We shall content ourselves for the present with mentioning a few of the principal. And let one thing be remembered by the reader. When item after item of the enumeration passes before him, and he finds one fact after another which he has been accustomed to include among the necessities of nature urged as an accusation against social institutions, he is not entitled to cry unfairness, and to protest that the evils complained of are inherent in Man and Society, and are such as no arrangements can remedy. To assert this would be to beg the very question at issue. No one is more ready than Socialists to admit—they affirm it indeed much more decidedly than truth warrants—that the evils they complain of are irremediable in the present constitution of society. They propose to consider whether some other form of society may be devised which would not be liable to those evils, or would be liable to them in a much less degree. Those who object to the present order of society, considered as a whole, and who accept as an alternative the possibility of a total change, have a right to set down all the evils which at present exist in society as part of their case, whether these are apparently attributable to social arrangements or not, provided they do not flow from physical laws which human power is not adequate, or human knowledge has not yet learned, to counteract. Moral evils, and such physical evils as would be remedied if all persons did as they ought, are fairly chargeable against the state of society which admits of them; and are valid as arguments until it is shown that any other state of society would involve an equal or greater amount of such evils. In the opinion of Socialists, the present arrangements of society in respect to Property and the Production and Distribution of Wealth, are, as means to the general good, a total failure. They say that there is an enormous mass of evil which these arrangements do not succeed in preventing; that the good, either moral or physical, which they realize is wretchedly small compared with the amount of exertion employed, and that even this small amount of good is brought about by means which are full of pernicious consequences, moral and physical.

First among existing social evils may be mentioned the evil of Poverty. The institution of Property is upheld and commended principally as being the means by which labor and frugality are insured their reward, and mankind enabled to emerge from indigence. It may be so; most Socialists allow that it has been so in earlier periods of history. But if the institution can do nothing more or better in this respect than it has hitherto done, its capabilities, they affirm, are very insignificant. What proportion of the population, in the most civilized countries of Europe, enjoy in their own persons anything worth naming of the benefits of property? It may be said, that but for property in the hands of their employers they would be without daily bread; but, though this be conceded, at least their daily bread is all that they have; and that often in insufficient quantity; almost always of inferior quality; and with no assurance of continuing to have it at all; an immense proportion of the industrious classes being at some period or other of their lives (and all being liable to become) dependent, at least temporarily, on legal or voluntary charity. Any attempt to depict the miseries of indigence, or to estimate the proportion of mankind who in the most advanced countries are habitually given up during their whole existence to its physical and moral sufferings, would be superfluous here. This may be left to philanthropists, who have painted these miseries in colors sufficiently strong. Suffice it to say that the condition of numbers in civilized Europe, and even in England and France, is more wretched than that of most tribes of savages who are known to us.

It may be said that of this hard lot no one has any reason to complain, because it befalls those only who are outstripped by others, from inferiority of energy or of prudence. This, even were it true, would be a very small alleviation of the evil. If some Nero or Domitian were to require a hundred persons to run a race for their lives, on condition that the fifty or twenty who came in hindmost should be put to death, it would not be any diminution of the injustice that the strongest or nimblest would, except through some untoward accident, be certain to escape. The misery and the crime would be that any were put to death at all. So in the economy of society; if there be any who suffer physical privation or moral degradation, whose bodily necessities are either not satisfied or satisfied in a manner which only brutish creatures can be content with, this, though not necessarily the crime of society, is *pro tanto* a failure of the social arrangements. And to assert as a mitigation of the evil that those who thus suffer are the weaker members of the community, morally or physically, is to add insult to misfortune. Is weakness a justification of suffering? Is it not, on the contrary, an irresistible claim upon every human being for protection against suffering? If the minds and feelings of the prosperous were in a right state, would they accept their prosperity if for the sake of it even one person near them was, for any other cause than voluntary fault, excluded from obtaining a desirable existence?

One thing there is, which if it could be affirmed truly, would relieve social institutions from any share in the responsibility of these evils. Since the human race has no means of enjoyable existence, or of existence at all, but what it derives from its own labor and abstinence, there would be no ground for complaint against society if every one who was willing to undergo a fair share of this labor and abstinence could attain a fair share of the fruits. But is this the fact? Is it not the reverse of the fact? The reward, instead of being proportioned to the labor and abstinence of the individual, is almost in an inverse ratio to it: those who receive the least, labor and abstain the most. Even the idle, reckless, and ill-conducted poor, those who are said with most justice to have themselves to blame for their condition, often undergo much more and severer labor, not only than those who are born to pecuniary independence, but than almost any of the more highly remunerated of those who earn their subsistence; and even the inadequate self-control exercised by the industrious poor costs them more sacrifice and more effort than is almost ever required from the more favored members of society. The very idea of distributive justice, or of any proportionality between success and merit, or between success and exertion, is in the present state of society so manifestly chimerical as to be relegated to the regions of romance. It is true that the lot of individuals is not wholly independent of their virtue and intelligence; these do really tell in their favor, but far less than many other things in which there is no merit at all. The most powerful of all the determining circumstances is birth. The great majority are what they were born to be. Some are born rich without work, others are born to a position in which they can become rich *by* work, the great majority are born to hard work and poverty throughout life, numbers to indigence. Next to birth the chief cause of success in life is accident and opportunity. When a person not born to riches succeeds in acquiring them, his own industry and dexterity have generally contributed to the result; but industry and dexterity would not have sufficed unless there had also been a concurrence of occasions and chances which falls to the lot of only a small number. If persons are helped in their worldly career by their virtues, so are they, and perhaps quite as often, by their vices: by servility and sycophancy, by hard-hearted and close-fisted selfishness, by the permitted lies and tricks of trade, by gambling speculations, not seldom by downright knavery. Energies and talents are of much more avail for success in life than virtues; but if one man succeeds by employing energy and talent in something generally useful, another thrives by exercising the same qualities in out-generaling and ruining a rival. It is as much as any moralist ventures to assert, that, other circumstances being given, honesty is the best policy, and that with parity of advantages an honest person has better chances than a rogue. Even this in many stations and circumstances of life is questionable; anything more than this is out of the question. It cannot be pretended that honesty, as a means of success, tells for as much as a difference of one single step on the social ladder. The connection between fortune and conduct is mainly this, that there is a degree of bad conduct, or rather of some kinds of bad conduct, which suffices to ruin any amount of good fortune; but the converse is not true: in the situation of most people no degree whatever of good conduct can be counted upon for raising them in the world, without the aid of fortunate accidents.

These evils, then—great poverty, and that poverty very little connected with desert—are the first grand failure of the existing arrangements of society. The second is human misconduct; crime, vice, and folly, with all the sufferings which follow in their train. For, nearly all the forms of misconduct, whether committed towards ourselves or towards others, may be traced to one of three causes: Poverty and its temptations in the many; Idleness and *désoeuvrement* in the few whose circumstances do not compel them to work; bad education, or want of education, in both. The first two must be allowed to be at least failures in the social arrangements, the last is now almost universally admitted to be the fault of those arrangements—it may almost be said the crime. I am speaking loosely and in the rough, for a minuter analysis of the sources of faults of character and errors of conduct would establish far more conclusively the filiation which connects them with a defective organization of society, though it would also show the reciprocal dependence of that faulty state of society on a backward state of the human mind.

At this point, in the enumeration of the evils of society, the mere levellers of former times usually stopped: but their more farsighted successors, the present Socialists, go farther. In their eyes the very foundation of human life as at present constituted, the very principle on which the production and repartition of all material products is now carried on, is essentially vicious and anti-social. It is the principle of individualism, competition, each one for himself and against all the rest. It is grounded on opposition of interests, not harmony of interests, and under it every one is required to find his place by a struggle, by pushing others back or being pushed back by them. Socialists consider this system of private war (as it may be termed) between every one and every one, especially fatal in an economical point of view and in a moral. Morally considered, its evils are obvious. It is the parent of envy, hatred, and all uncharitableness; it makes every one the natural enemy of all others who cross his path, and every one's path is constantly liable to be crossed. Under the present system hardly any one can gain except by the loss or disappointment of one or of many others. In a well-constituted community every one would be a gainer by every other person's successful exertions; while now we gain by each other's loss and lose by each other's gain, and our greatest gains come from the worst source of all, from death, the death of those who are nearest and should be dearest to us. In its purely economical operation the principle of individual competition receives an unqualified condemnation from the social reformers as in its moral. In the competition of laborers they see the cause of low wages; in the competition of producers the cause of ruin and bankruptcy; and both evils, they affirm, tend constantly to increase as population and wealth make progress; no person (they conceive) being benefited except the great proprietors of land, the holders of fixed money incomes, and a few great capitalists, whose wealth is gradually enabling them to undersell all other producers, to absorb the whole of the operations of industry into their own sphere, to drive from the market all employers of labor except themselves, and to convert the laborers into a kind of slaves or serfs, dependent on them for the means of support, and compelled to accept these on such terms as they choose to offer. Society, in short, is travelling onward, according to these speculators, towards a new feudality, that of the great capitalists.

As I shall have ample opportunity in future chapters to state my own opinion on these topics, and on many others connected with and subordinate to them, I shall now, without further preamble, exhibit the opinions of distinguished Socialists on the present arrangements of society, in a selection of passages from their published writings. For the present I desire to be considered as a mere reporter of the opinions of others. Hereafter it will appear how much of what I cite agrees or differs with my own sentiments.

The clearest, the most compact, and the most precise and specific statement of the case of the Socialists generally against the existing order of society in the economical department of human affairs, is to be found in the little work of M. Louis Blanc, *Organisation du Travail* [*The Organi-*

zation of Labor]. My first extracts, therefore, on this part of the subject, shall be taken from that treatise.

> Competition is for the people a system of extermination. Is the poor man a member of society, or an enemy to it? We ask for an answer.
>
> All around him he finds the soil preoccupied. Can he cultivate the earth for himself? No; for the right of the first occupant has become a right of property. Can he gather the fruits which the hand of God ripens on the path of man? No; for, like the soil, the fruits have been *appropriated*. Can he hunt or fish? No; for that is a right which is dependent upon the government. Can he draw water from a spring enclosed in a field? No; for the proprietor of the field is, in virtue of his right to the field, proprietor of the fountain. Can he, dying of hunger and thirst, stretch out his hands for the charity of his fellow-creatures? No; for there are laws against begging. Can he, exhausted by fatigue and without a refuge, lie down to sleep upon the pavement of the streets? No; for there are laws against vagabondage. Can he, flying from the cruel native land where everything is denied him, seek the means of living far from the place where life was given him? No; for it is not permitted to change your country except on certain conditions which the poor man cannot fulfill.
>
> What, then, can the unhappy man do? He will say, "I have hands to work with, I have intelligence, I have youth, I have strength; take all this, and in return give me a morsel of bread." This is what the working men do say. But even here the poor man may be answered, "I have no work to give you." What is he to do then?

* * * * * *

What is competition from the point of view of the workman? It is work put up to auction. A contractor wants a workman: three present themselves.—How much for your work?—Half-a-crown: I have a wife and children.—Well; and how much for yours?—Two shillings: I have no children, but I have a wife.—Very well; and now how much for you?—One and eightpence are enough for me; I am single. Then you shall have the work. It is done; the bargain is struck. And what are the other two workmen to do? It is to be hoped they will die quietly of hunger. But what if they take to thieving? Never fear; we have the police. To murder? We have got the hangman. As for the lucky one, his triumph is only temporary. Let a fourth workman make his appearance, strong enough to fast every other day, and his price will run down still lower; then there will be a new outcast, a new recruit for the prison perhaps!

Will it be said that these melancholy results are exaggerated; that at all events they are only possible when there is not enough work for the hands that seek employment? But I ask, in answer, Does the principle of competition contain, by chance, within itself any method by which this murderous disproportion is to be avoided? If one branch of industry is in want of hands, who can answer for it that, in the confusion created by universal competition, another is not overstocked? And if, out of thirty-four millions of men, twenty are really reduced to theft for a living, this would suffice to condemn the principle.

But who is so blind as not to see that under the system of unlimited competition, the continual fall of wages is no exceptional circumstance, but a necessary and general fact? Has the population a limit which it cannot exceed? Is it possible for us to say to industry—

industry given up to the accidents of individual egotism and fertile in ruin—can we say, "Thus far shalt thou go, and no farther?" The population increases constantly: tell the poor mother to become sterile, and blaspheme the God who made her fruitful, for if you do not the lists will soon become too narrow for the combatants. A machine is invented: command it to be broken, and anathematize science, for if you do not, the thousand workmen whom the new machine deprives of work will knock at the door of the neighboring workshop, and lower the wages of their companions. Thus systematic lowering of wages, ending in the driving out of a certain number of workmen, is the inevitable effect of unlimited competition. It is an industrial system by means of which the working classes are forced to exterminate one another.

* * * * * *

If there is an undoubted fact, it is that the increase of population is much more rapid among the poor than among the rich. According to the *Statistics of European Population,* the births at Paris are only one-thirty-second of the population in the rich quarters, while in the others they rise to one-twenty-sixth. This disproportion is a general fact, and M. de Sismondi, in his work on Political Economy, has explained it by the impossibility for the workmen of hopeful prudence. Those only who feel themselves assured of the morrow can regulate the number of their children according to their income; he who lives from day to day is under the yoke of a mysterious fatality, to which he sacrifices his children as he was sacri-

> ficed to it himself. It is true the workhouses exist, menacing society with an inundation of beggars—what way is there of escaping from the cause? . . . It is clear that any society where the means of subsistence increase less rapidly than the numbers of the population, is a society on the brink of an abyss . . . . Competition produces destitution; this is a fact shown by statistics. Destitution is fearfully prolific; this is shown by statistics. The fruitfulness of the poor throws upon society unhappy creatures who have the need of work and cannot find it; this is shown by statistics. At this point society is reduced to a choice between killing the poor or maintaining them gratuitously—between atrocity or folly.[1]

So much for the poor. We now pass to the middle classes.

> According to the political economists of the school of Adam Smith and Léon Say, *cheapness* is the word in which may be summed up the advantages of unlimited competition. But why persist in considering the effect of cheapness with a view only to the momentary advantage of the consumer? Cheapness is advantageous to the consumer at the cost of introducing the seeds of ruinous anarchy among the producers. Cheapness is, so to speak, the hammer with which the rich among the producers crush their poorer rivals. Cheapness is the trap into which the daring speculators entice the hard-workers. Cheapness is the sentence of death to the producer on a small scale who has no money to invest in the purchase of machinery that his rich rivals can easily procure. Cheapness is the

great instrument in the hands of monopoly; it absorbs the small manufacturer, the small shopkeeper, the small proprietor; it is, in one word, the destruction of the middle classes for the advantage of a few industrial oligarchs.

Ought we, then, to consider cheapness as a curse? No one would attempt to maintain such an absurdity. But it is the speciality of wrong principles to turn good into evil and to corrupt all things. Under the system of competition cheapness is only a provisional and fallacious advantage. It is maintained only so long as there is a struggle; no sooner have the rich competitors driven out their poorer rivals than prices rise. Competition leads to monopoly, for the same reason cheapness leads to high prices. Thus, what has been made use of as a weapon in the contest between the producers, sooner or later becomes a cause of impoverishment among the consumers. And if to this cause we add the others we have already enumerated, first among which must be ranked the inordinate increase of the population, we shall be compelled to recognize the impoverishment of the mass of the consumers as a direct consequence of competition.

But, on the other hand, this very competition which tends to dry up the sources of demand, urges production to over-supply. The confusion produced by the universal struggle prevents each producer from knowing the state of the market. He must work in the dark and trust to chance for a sale. Why should he check the supply, especially as he can throw any loss on the workman whose wages are so preeminently liable to rise and fall? Even when production is carried on at a loss the manufacturers still often carry it on, because they will not let their machinery, &c., stand idle, or risk the loss of raw material, or lose their customers; and because productive industry as carried on under the competitive system being nothing less than a game of chance, the gambler will not lose his chance of a lucky stroke.

Thus, and we cannot too often insist upon it, competition necessarily tends to increase supply and to diminish consumption; its tendency therefore is precisely the opposite of what is sought by economic science; hence it is not merely oppressive but foolish as well.

* * * * * *

And in all this, in order to avoid dwelling on truths which have become commonplaces and sound declamatory from their very truth, we have said nothing of the frightful moral corruption which industry, organized, or more properly speaking disorganized as it is at the present day, has introduced among the middle classes. Everything has become venal, and competition invades even the domain of thought.

The factory crushing the workshop; the showy establishment absorbing the humble shop; the artisan who is his own master replaced by the day-laborer; cultivation by the plough superseding that by the spade, and bringing the poor man's field under disgraceful homage to the money-lender; bankruptcies multiplied; manufacturing industry transformed by the ill-regulated extension of credit into a system of gambling where no one, not even the rogue, can be sure of winning; in short a vast confusion calculated to arouse jealousy, mistrust, and hatred, and to stifle, little by little, all generous aspirations, all faith, self-sacrifice, and poetry—such is the hideous but only too faithful picture of the results obtained by the application of the principle of competition.[2]

The Fourierists, through their principal organ, M. Considérant, enumerate the evils of the existing civilization in the following order:

1. It employs an enormous quantity of labor and of human power unproductively, or in the work of destruction.

> In the first place there is the army, which in France, as in all other countries, absorbs the healthiest and strongest men, a large number of the most talented and intelligent, and a considerable part of the public revenue. . . . The existing state of society develops in its impure atmosphere innumerable outcasts, whose labor is not merely unproductive, but actually destructive: adventurers, prostitutes, people with no acknowledged means of living, beggars, convicts, swindlers, thieves, and others whose number tends rather to increase than to diminish. . . .
>
> To the list of unproductive labor fostered by our state of Society must be added that of the judicature and of the bar, of the courts and magistrates, the police, gaolers, executioners, &c.—functions indispensable to the state of society as it is.
>
> Also people of what is called "good society"; those who pass their lives in doing nothing; idlers of all ranks.
>
> Also the numberless custom-house officials, tax-gatherers, bailiffs, excisemen; in short, all that army of men which overlooks, brings to account, takes, but produces nothing.
>
> Also the labors of sophists, philosophers, metaphysicians, political men, working in mistaken directions, who do nothing to advance science, and produce nothing but disturbance and sterile discussions; the verbiage of advo-

cates, pleaders, witnesses, &c.

And finally all the operations of commerce, from those of the bankers and brokers, down to those of the grocer behind his counter.[3]

Secondly, they assert that even the industry and powers which in the present system are devoted to production, do not produce more than a small portion of what they might produce if better employed and directed:

Who with any good-will and reflection will not see how much the want of coherence—the disorder, the want of combination, the parcelling out of labor and leaving it wholly to individual action without any organization, without any large or general views—are causes which limit the possibilities of production and destroy, or at least waste, our means of action? Does not disorder give birth to poverty, as order and good management give birth to riches? Is not want of combination a source of weakness, as combination is a source of strength? And who can say that industry, whether agricultural, domestic, manufacturing, scientific, artistic, or commercial, is organized at the present day either in the state or in municipalities? Who can say that all the work which is carried on in any of these departments is executed in subordination to any general views, or with foresight, economy, and order? Or, again, who can say that it is possible in our present state of society to develop, by a good education, all the faculties bestowed by nature on each of its members; to employ each one in functions which he would like, which he would be the most capable of, and which, therefore, he could carry on with the greatest advantage to himself and to others? Has it even been so much as attempted to solve the problems presented by varieties of character so as to regulate and harmonize the varieties of employments in accordance with natural aptitudes? Alas! The Utopia of the most ardent philanthropists is to teach reading and writing to twenty-five millions of the French people! And in the present state of things we may defy them to succeed even in that!

And is it not a strange spectacle, too, and one which cries out in condemnation of us, to see this state of society where the soil is badly cultivated, and sometimes not cultivated at all; where man is ill lodged, ill clothed, and yet where whole masses are continually in need of work, and pining in misery because they cannot find it? Of a truth we are forced to acknowledge that if the nations are poor and starving it is not because nature has denied the means of producing wealth, but because of the anarchy and disorder in our employment of those means; in other words, it is because society is wretchedly constituted and labor unorganized.

But this is not all, and you will have but a faint conception of the evil if you do not consider that to all these vices of society, which dry up the sources of wealth and prosperity, must be added the struggle, the discord, the war, in short, under many names and many forms which society cherishes and cultivates between the individuals that compose it. These struggles and discords correspond to radical oppositions—deep-seated antinomies between the various interests. Exactly in so far as you are able to establish classes and categories within the nation; in so far, also, you will have opposition of interests and internal warfare either avowed or secret, even if you take into consideration the industrial system only.[4]

One of the leading ideas of this school is the wastefulness and at the same time the immorality of the existing arrangements for distributing the produce of the country among the various consumers, the enormous superfluity in point of number of the agents of distribution, the merchants, dealers, shopkeepers and their innumerable employees, and the depraving character of such a distribution of occupations.

> It is evident that the interest of the trader is opposed to that of the consumer and of the producer. Has he not bought cheap and undervalued as much as possible in all his dealings with the producer, the very same article which, vaunting its excellence, he sells to you as dear as he can? Thus the interest of the commercial body, collectively and individually, is contrary to that of the producer and of the consumer—that is to say, to the interest of the whole body of society.
>
> * * * * * *
>
> The trader is a go-between, who profits by the general anarchy and the nonorganization of industry. The trader buys up products, he buys up everything; he owns and detains everything, in such sort that:
>
> 1stly. He holds both Production and Consumption *under his yoke,* because both must come to him either finally for the products to be consumed, or at first for the raw materials to be worked up. Commerce with all its methods of buying, and of raising and lowering prices, its innumerable devices, and its holding everything in the

hands of *middle-men,* levies toll right and left: it despotically gives the law to Production and Consumption, of which it ought to be only the subordinate.

2ndly. It robs society by its *enormous profits*—profits levied upon the consumer and the producer, and altogether out of proportion to the services rendered, for which a twentieth of the persons actually employed would be sufficient.

3rdly. It robs society by the subtraction of its productive forces; taking off from productive labor nineteen-twentieths of the agents of trade who are mere parasites. Thus, not only does commerce rob society by appropriating an exorbitant share of the common wealth, but also by considerably diminishing the productive energy of the human beehive. The great majority of traders would return to productive work if a rational system of commercial organization were substituted for the inextricable chaos of the present state of things.

4thly. It robs society by the *adulteration* of products, pushed at the present day beyond all bounds. And in fact, if a hundred grocers establish themselves in a town where before there were only twenty, it is plain that people will not begin to consume five times as many groceries. Hereupon the hundred virtuous grocers have to dispute between them the profits which before were honestly made by the twenty; competition obliges them to make it up at the expense of the consumer, either by raising the prices as sometimes happens, or by adulterating the goods as always happens. In such a state of things there is an end to good faith. Inferior or adulterated goods are sold for articles of good quality whenever the credulous customer is not too experienced to be deceived. And when the customer has been thoroughly imposed upon, the trading conscience consoles itself by saying, "I state my price; people can take or leave; no one is obliged to buy." The losses imposed on the consumers by the bad quality or the adulteration of goods are incalculable.

5thly. It robs society by *accumulations,* artificial or not, in consequence of which vast quantities of goods, collected in one place, are damaged and destroyed for want of a sale. Fourier (Th. des Quat. Mouv., p. 334, 1st ed.) says: "The fundamental principle of the commercial systems, that of *leaving full liberty to the merchants,* gives them absolute right of property over the goods in which they deal; they have the right to withdraw them altogether, to withhold or even to burn them, as happened more than once with the Oriental Company of Amsterdam, which publicly burnt stores of cinnamon in order to raise the price. What it did with cinnamon it would have done with corn; but for the fear of being stoned by the populace, it would have burnt some corn in order to sell the rest at four times its value. Indeed, it actually is of daily occurrence in ports, for provisions of grains to be thrown into the sea because the merchants have allowed them to rot while waiting for a rise. I myself, when I was a clerk, have had to superintend these infamous proceedings, and in one day caused to be thrown into the sea some forty thousand bushels of rice, which might have been sold at a fair profit had the withholder been less greedy of gain. It is society that bears the cost of this waste, which takes place daily under shelter of the philosophical maxim of *full liberty for the merchants.*"

6thly. Commerce robs society, moreover, by all the loss, damage, and waste that follows from the extreme scattering of products in millions of shops, and by the multiplication and complication of carriage.

7thly. It robs society by shameless and unlimited

usury—usury absolutely appalling. The trader carries on operations with fictitious capital, much higher in amount than his real capital. A trader with a capital of twelve hundred pounds will carry on operations, by means of bills and credit, on a scale of four, eight, or twelve thousand pounds. Thus he draws from capital *which he does not possess,* usurious interest, out of all proportion with the capital he actually owns.

8thly. It robs society by innumerable *bankruptcies,* for the daily accidents of our commercial system, political events, and any kind of disturbance, must usher in a day when the trader, having incurred obligations beyond his means, is no longer able to meet them; his failure, whether fraudulent or not, must be a severe blow to his creditors. The bankruptcy of some entails that of others, so that bankruptcies follow one upon another, causing widespread ruin. And it is always the producer and the consumer who suffer; for commerce, considered as a whole, does not produce wealth, and invests very little in proportion to the wealth which passes through its hands. How many are the manufactures crushed by these blows! how many fertile sources of wealth dried up by these devices, with all their disastrous consequences!

The producer furnishes the goods, the consumer the money. Trade furnishes credit, founded on little or no actual capital, and the different members of the commercial body are in no way responsible for one another. This, in a few words, is the whole theory of the thing.

9thly. Commerce robs society by the *independence* and *irresponsibility* which permits it to buy at the epochs when the producers are forced to sell and compete with one another, in order to procure money for their rent and necessary expenses of production. When the markets are overstocked and goods cheap, trade purchases. Then it creates a rise, and by this simple maneuver despoils both producer and consumer.

10thly. It robs society by a considerable *drawing off* of *capital,* which will return to productive industry when commerce plays its proper subordinate part, and is only an agency carrying on transactions between the producers (more or less distant) and the great centers of consumption—the communistic societies. Thus the capital engaged in the speculations of commerce (which, small as it is, compared to the immense wealth which passes through its hands, consists nevertheless of sums enormous in themselves), would return to stimulate production if commerce was deprived of the intermediate property in goods, and their distribution became a matter of administrative organization. Stock-jobbing is the most odious form of this vice of commerce.

11thly. It robs society by the *monopolizing* or buying up of raw materials. "For" (says Fourier, Th. des Quat. Mouv., p. 359, 1st ed.), "the rise in price on articles that are bought up, is borne ultimately by the consumer, although in the first place by the manufacturers, who, being obliged to keep up their establishments, must make pecuniary sacrifices, and manufacture at small profits in the hope of better days; and it is often long before they can repay themselves the rise in prices which the monopolizer has compelled them to support in the first instance. . . ."

In short, all these vices, besides many others which I omit, are multiplied by the extreme complication of mercantile affairs; for products do not pass once only through the greedy clutches of commerce; there are some which pass and repass twenty or thirty times before reaching the consumer. In the first place, the raw material passes through the grasp of commerce before reaching the manufacturer who first works it up; then it returns to commerce to be sent out again to be worked up in a second form; and so on until it receives its final shape. Then it passes into the hands of merchants, who sell to the wholesale dealers, and these to the great retail dealers of towns, and these again to the little dealers and to the country shops; and each time that it changes hands, it leaves something behind it.

. . . One of my friends who was lately exploring the Jura, where much working in metal is done, had occasion to enter the house of a peasant who was a manufacturer of shovels. He asked the price. "Let us come to an understanding," answered the poor laborer, not an economist at all, but a man of common sense; "I sell them for 8*d.* to the trade, which retails them at 1*s.* 8*d.* in the towns. If you could find a means of opening a direct communication between the workman and the consumer, you might have them for 1*s.* 2*d.*, and we should each gain 6*d.* by the transaction."[5]

To a similar effect Owen, in the *Book of the New Moral World,* part 2, chap. iii.

The principle now in practice is to induce a large portion of society to devote their lives to distribute wealth upon a large, a medium, and a small scale, and to have it conveyed from place to place in larger or smaller quantities, to meet the means and wants of various divisions of society and individuals, as they are now situated in cities, towns, villages, and country places. This principle of distribution makes a class in society whose business it is to *buy from* some parties and to *sell to* others. By this proceeding they are placed under circumstances which induce them to endeavor to buy at what appears at the time a low price in the market, and to sell again at the greatest permanent profit which they can obtain. Their real object being to get as much profit as gain between the seller to, and the buyer from them, as can be effected in their transactions.

There are innumerable errors in principle and evils in practice which necessarily proceed from this mode of distributing the wealth of society.

1st. A general class of distributors is formed, whose interest is separated from, and apparently opposed to, that of the individual from whom they buy and to whom they sell.

2nd. Three classes of distributors are made, the small, the medium, and the large buyers and sellers; or the retailers, the wholesale dealers, and the extensive merchants.

3rd. Three classes of buyers thus created constitute the small, the medium, and the large purchasers.

By this arrangement into various classes of buyers and sellers, the parties are easily trained to learn that they have separate and opposing interests, and different ranks and stations in society. An inequality of feeling and condition is thus created and maintained, with all the servility and pride which these unequal arrangements are sure to produce. The parties are regularly trained in a general system of deception, in order that they may be the more successful in buying cheap and selling dear.

The smaller sellers acquire habits of injurious idleness, waiting often for hours for customers. And this evil is experienced to a considerable extent even amongst the class of wholesale dealers.

There are, also, by this arrangement, many more establishments for selling than are necessary in the villages, towns, and cities; and a very large capital is thus wasted without benefit to society. And from their number opposed to each other all over the country to obtain customers, they endeavor to undersell each other, and are therefore continually endeavoring to injure the producer by the establishment of what are called cheap shops and warehouses; and to support their character the master of his servants must be continually on the watch to buy bargains, that is, to procure wealth for less than the cost of its production.

The distributors, small, medium, and large, have all to be supported by the producers, and the greater the number of the former compared with the latter, the greater will be the burden which the producer has to sustain; for as the number of distributors increases, the accumulation of wealth must decrease, and more must be required from the producer.

The distributors of wealth, under the present system, are a dead weight upon the producers, and are most active demoralizers of society. Their dependent condition, at the commencement of their task, teaches or induces them to be servile to their customers, and to continue to be so as long as they are accumulating wealth by their cheap buying and dear selling. But when they have secured sufficient to be what they imagine to be an independence—to live without business—they are too often filled with a most ignorant pride, and become insolent to their dependents.

The arrangement is altogether a most improvident one for society, whose interest it is to produce the greatest amount of wealth of the best qualities; while the existing system of distribution is not only to withdraw great numbers from producing to become distributors, but to add to the cost of the consumer all the expense of a most wasteful and extravagant distribution; the distribution costing to the consumer many times the price of the original cost of the wealth purchased.

Then, by the position in which the seller is placed by his created desire for gain on the one hand, and the competition he meets with from opponents selling similar productions on the other, he is strongly tempted to deteriorate the articles which he has for sale; and when these are provisions, either of home production or of foreign importation, the effects upon the health, and consequent comfort and happiness of the consumers, are often most injurious, and productive of much premature death, especially among the working classes, who, in this respect, are perhaps made to be the greatest sufferers, by purchasing the inferior or low-priced articles. . . .

The expense of thus distributing wealth in Great Britain and Ireland, including transit from place to place, and all the agents directly and indirectly engaged in this department is, perhaps, little short of one hundred millions annually, without taking into consideration the deterioration of the quality of many of the articles constituting this wealth, by carriage, and by being divided into small quantities, and kept in improper stores and places, in which the atmosphere is unfavorable to the keeping of such articles in a tolerably good, and much less in the best, condition for use.

In further illustration of the contrariety of interests between person and person, class and class, which pervades the present constitution of society, M. Considérant adds:

> If the wine-growers wish for free trade, this freedom ruins the producer of corn, the manufacturers of iron, of cloth, of cotton, and—we are compelled to add—the smuggler and the customs' officer. If it is the interest of the consumer that machines should be invented which lower prices by rendering production less costly, these same machines throw out of work thousands of workmen who do not know how to, and cannot at once, find other work. Here, then, again is one of the innumerable *vicious circles* of civilization . . . for there are a thousand facts which prove cumulatively that in our existing social system the introduction of any good brings always along with it some evil.
>
> In short, if we go lower down and come to vulgar details, we find that it is the interest of the tailor, the shoemaker, and the hatter that coats, shoes, and hats should be soon worn out; that the glazier profits by the hail-storms which break windows; that the mason and the architect profit by fires; the lawyer is enriched by lawsuits; the doctor by disease; the wine-seller by drunkenness; the prostitute by debauchery. And what a disaster would it be for the judges, the police, and the gaolers, as well as for the barristers and the solicitors, and all the lawyers' clerks if crimes, offenses, and lawsuits were all at once to come to an end![6]

The following is one of the cardinal points of this school:

> Add to all this, that civilization, which sows dissension and war on every side; which employs a great part

of its powers in unproductive labor, or even in destruction; which furthermore diminishes the public wealth by the unnecessary friction and discord it introduces into industry; add to all this, I say, that this same social system has for its special characteristic to produce a repugnance for work—a disgust for labor.

Everywhere you hear the laborer, the artisan, the clerk complain of his position and his occupation, while they long for the time when they can retire from work imposed upon them by necessity. To be repugnant, to have for its motive and pivot nothing but the fear of starvation, is the great, the fatal, characteristic of civilized labor. The civilized workman is condemned to penal servitude. So long as productive labor is so organized that instead of being associated with pleasure it is associated with pain, weariness and dislike, it will always happen that all will avoid it who are able. With few exceptions, those only will consent to work who are compelled to it by want. Hence the most numerous classes, the artificers of social wealth, the active and direct creators of all comfort and luxury, will always be condemned to touch closely on poverty and hunger; they will always be the slaves to ignorance and degradation; they will continue to be always that huge herd of mere beasts of burden whom we see ill-grown, decimated by disease, bowed down in the great workshop of society over the plough or over the counter, that they may prepare the delicate food, and the sumptuous enjoyments of the upper and idle classes.

So long as no method of attractive labor has been devised, it will continue to be true that "there must be many poor in order that there may be a few rich"; a mean and hateful saying, which we hear every day quoted as an eternal truth from the mouths of people who call themselves Christians or philosophers! It is very easy to

> understand that oppression, trickery, and especially poverty, are the permanent and fatal appanage of every state of society characterized by the dislike of work, for, in this case, there is nothing but poverty that will force men to labor. And the proof of this is, that if every one of all the workers were to become suddenly rich, nineteen-twentieths of all the work now done would be abandoned.[7]

In the opinion of the Fourierists, the tendency of the present order of society is to a concentration of wealth in the hands of a comparatively few immensely rich individuals or companies, and the reduction of all the rest of the community into a complete dependence on them. This was termed by Fourier *la féodalité industrielle.*

> "This feudalism," says M. Considérant, "would be constituted as soon as the largest part of the industrial and territorial property of the nation belongs to a minority which absorbs all its revenues, while the great majority, chained to the work-bench or laboring on the soil, must be content to gnaw the pittance which is cast to them."[8]

This disastrous result is to be brought about partly by the mere progress of competition, as sketched in our previous extract by M. Louis Blanc; assisted by the progress of national debts, which M. Considérant regards as mortgages of the whole land and capital of the country, of which "les capitalistes prêteurs" become, in a greater and greater measure, co-proprietors, receiving without labor or risk an increasing portion of the revenues.

NOTES

1. See Louis Blanc, "Organisation du Travail," 4me édition, pp. 6, 11, 53, 57.
2. See Louis Blanc, "Organisation du Travail," pp. 58-61, 65-66, 4me édition. Paris, 1845.
3. See Considérant, "Destinée Sociale," tome i. pp. 35, 36, 37, 3me éd. Paris, 1848.
4. See "Destinée Sociale," par V. Considérant, tome i. pp. 38-40.
5. See Considérant, "Destinée Sociale," tome i. pp. 43-51, 3me édition, Paris, 1848.
6. Considérant, "Destinée Sociale," tome i., pp. 59, 60.
7. Considérant, "Destinée Sociale," tome i., pp. 60, 61.
8. "Destinée Sociale," tome i., p. 134.

Three

The Socialist Objections to the Present Order of Society Examined

It is impossible to deny that the considerations brought to notice in the preceding chapter make out a frightful case either against the existing order of society, or against the position of man himself in this world. How much of the evils should be referred to the one, and how much to the other, is the principal theoretic question which has to be resolved. But the strongest case is susceptible of exaggeration; and it will have been evident to many readers, even from the passages I have quoted, that such exaggeration is not wanting in the representations of the ablest and most candid Socialists. Though much of their allegations is unanswerable, not a little is the result of errors in political economy; by which, let me say once for all, I do not mean the rejection of any practical rules of policy which have been laid down by political economists, I mean ignorance of economic facts, and of the causes by which the economic phenomena of society as it is, are actually determined.

In the first place, it is unhappily true that the wages of ordinary labor, in all the countries of Europe, are wretchedly insufficient to supply the physical and moral necessities of the population in any tolerable measure. But, when it is further alleged that even this insufficient remuneration has a tendency to diminish; that there is, in the words of M. Louis Blanc, *une baisse continue des salaires;* the assertion is in opposition to all accurate information, and to many notorious facts. It has yet to be proved that there is any country in the civilized world where the ordinary wages of labor, estimated either in money or in articles of consumption, are declining; while in many they are, on the whole, on the increase; and an increase which is becoming, not slower, but more rapid. There are, occasionally, branches of industry which are being gradually superseded by something else, and, in those, until production accommodates itself to demand, wages are depressed; which is an evil, but a temporary one, and would admit of great alleviation even in the present system of social economy. A diminution thus produced of the reward of labor in some particular employment is the effect and the evidence of increased remuneration, or of a new source of remuneration, in some other; the total and the average remuneration being undiminished, or even increased. To make out an appearance of diminution in the rate of wages in any leading branch of industry, it is always found necessary to compare some month or year of special and temporary depression at the present time, with the average rate, or even some exceptionally high rate, at an earlier time. The vicissitudes are no doubt a great evil, but they were as frequent and as severe in former periods of economical history as now. The greater scale of the transactions, and the greater number of persons involved in each fluctuation, may make the fluctuation appear greater, but though a larger population affords more sufferers, the evil does not weigh heavier on each of them individually. There is much evidence of improvement, and none, that is at all trustworthy, of deterioration, in the mode of living of the laboring population of the countries of Europe; when there is any appearance to the contrary it is local or partial, and can always be traced either to the pressure of some temporary calamity, or to some bad law or unwise act of government which admits of being corrected, while the permanent causes all operate in the direction of improvement.

M. Louis Blanc, therefore, while showing himself much more enlightened than the older school of levellers and democrats, inasmuch as he recognizes the connection between low wages and the over-rapid increase of population, appears to have fallen into the same error which was at first committed by Malthus and his followers, that of supposing that because population has a greater power of increase than subsistence, its pressure upon subsistence must be always growing more severe. The difference is that the early Malthusians thought this an irrepressible tendency, while M. Louis Blanc thinks that it can be repressed, but only under a system of Communism. It is a great point gained for truth when it comes to be seen that the tendency to over-population is a fact which Communism, as well as the existing order of society, would have to deal with. And it is much to be rejoiced at that this necessity is admitted by the most considerable chiefs of all existing schools of Socialism. Owen and Fourier, no less than M. Louis Blanc, admitted it, and claimed for their respective systems a preeminent power of dealing with this difficulty. However this may be, experience shows that in the existing state of society the pressure of population on subsistence, which is the principal cause of low wages, though a great, is not an increasing evil; on the contrary, the progress of all that is called civilization has a tendency to diminish it, partly by the more rapid increase of the means of employing and maintaining labor, partly by the increased facilities opened to labor for transporting itself to new countries and unoccupied fields of employment, and partly by a general improvement in the intelligence and prudence of the population. This progress, no doubt, is slow; but it is much that such progress should take place at all, while we are still only in the first stage of that public movement for the education of the whole people, which when more advanced must add greatly to the force of all the two causes of improvement specified above. It is, of course, open to discussion what form of society has the greatest power of dealing successfully with the pressure of population on subsistence, and on this question there is much to be said for Socialism; what was long thought to be its weakest point will, perhaps, prove to be one of its strongest. But it has no just claim to be considered as the sole means of preventing the general and growing degradation of the mass of mankind through the peculiar tendency of poverty to produce over-population. Society as at present constituted is not descending into that abyss, but gradually, though slowly, rising out of it, and this improvement is likely to be progressive if bad laws do not interfere with it.

Next, it must be observed that Socialists generally, and even the most enlightened of them, have a very imperfect and one-sided notion of the operation of competition. They see half its effects, and overlook the other half; they regard it as an agency for grinding down everyone's remuneration—for obliging everyone to accept less wages for his labor, or a less price for his commodities, which would be true only if everyone had to dispose of his labor or his commodities to some great monopolist, and the competition were all on one side. They forget that competition is a cause of high prices and values as well as of low; that the buyers of labor and of commodities compete with one another as well as the sellers; and that if it is competition which keeps the prices of labor and commodities as low as they are, it is competition which prevents them from falling still lower. In truth, when competition is perfectly free on both sides, its tendency is not specially either to raise or to lower the price of articles, but to equalize it; to level inequalities of remuneration, and to reduce all to a general average, a result which, in so far as realized (no doubt very imperfectly), is, on Socialistic principles, desirable. But if, disregarding for the time that part of the effects of competition which consists in keeping up prices, we fix our attention on its effect in keeping them down, and contemplate this effect in reference solely to the interest of the laboring classes, it would seem that if competition keeps down wages, and so gives a motive to the laboring classes to withdraw the labor market from the full influence of competition, if they can, it must on the other hand have credit for keeping down the prices of the articles on which wages are expended, to the great advantage of those who depend on wages. To meet this consideration Socialists, as we said in our quotation from M. Louis Blanc, are reduced to affirm that the low prices of commodities produced by competition are delusive and lead in the end to higher prices than before, because when the richest competitor has got rid of all his rivals, he commands the market and can demand any price he pleases. Now, the commonest experience shows that this state of things, under really free competition, is wholly imaginary. The richest competitor neither does nor can get rid of all his rivals, and establish himself in exclusive possession of the market; and it is not the fact that any important branch of industry or commerce formerly divided among many has become, or shows any tendency to become, the monopoly of a few.

The kind of policy described is sometimes possible where, as in the case of railways, the only competition possible is between two or three great companies, the operations being on too vast a scale to be within the reach of individual capitalists; and this is one of the reasons why businesses which require to be carried on by great joint-stock enterprises cannot be trusted to competition, but, when not reserved by the State to itself, ought to be carried on under conditions prescribed, and, from time to time, varied by the State, for the purpose of insuring to the public a cheaper supply of its wants than would be afforded by private interest in the absence of sufficient competition. But in the ordinary branches of industry no one rich competitor has it in his power to drive out all the smaller ones. Some businesses show a tendency to pass out of the hands of many small producers or dealers into a smaller number of larger ones; but the cases in which this happens are those in which the possession of a larger capital permits the adoption of more powerful machinery, more efficient by more expensive processes, or a better organized and more economical mode of carrying on business, and thus enables the large dealer legitimately and permanently to supply the commodity cheaper than can be done on the small scale; to the great advantage of the consumers, and therefore of the laboring classes, and diminishing, *pro tanto,* that waste of the resources of the community so much complained of by Socialists, the unnecessary multiplication of mere distributors, and of the various other classes whom Fourier calls the parasites of industry. When this change is effected, the larger capitalists, either individual or joint-stock, among which the business is divided, are seldom, if ever, in any considerable branch of commerce, so few as that competition shall not continue to act between them; so that the saving in cost, which enabled them to undersell the small dealers, continues afterwards, as at first, to be passed on, in lower prices, to their customers. The operation, therefore, of competition in keeping down the prices of commodities, including those on which wages are expended, is not illusive, but real, and, we may add, is a growing, not a declining, fact.

But there are other respects, equally important, in which the charges brought by Socialists against competition do not admit of so complete an answer. Competition is the best security for cheapness, but by no means a security for quality. In former times, when producers and consumers were less numerous, it was a security for both. The market was not large enough nor the means of publicity sufficient to enable a dealer to make a fortune by continually attracting new customers: his success depended on his retaining those that he had; and when a dealer furnished good articles, or when he did not, the fact was soon known to those whom it concerned, and he acquired a character for honest or dishonest dealing of more importance to him than the gain that would be made by cheating casual purchasers. But on the great scale of modern transactions, with the great multiplication of competition and the immense increase in the quantity of business competed for, dealers are so little dependent on permanent customers that character is much less essential to them, while there is also far less certainty of their obtaining the character they deserve. The low prices which a tradesman advertises are known, to a thousand for one who has discovered for himself or learned from others, that the bad quality of the goods is more than an equivalent for their cheapness; while at the same time the much greater fortunes now made by some dealers excite the cupidity of all, and the greed of rapid gain substitutes itself for the modest desire to make a living by their business. In this manner, as wealth increases and greater prizes seem to be within reach, more and more of a gambling spirit is introduced into commerce; and where this prevails not only are the simplest maxims of prudence disregarded, but all, even the most perilous, forms of pecuniary improbity receive a terrible stimulus. This is the meaning of what is called the intensity of modern competition. It is further to be mentioned that when this intensity has reached a certain height, and when a portion of the producers of an article or the dealers in it have resorted to any of the modes of fraud, such as adulteration, giving short measure, &c., of the increase of which there is now so much complaint, the temptation is immense on these to adopt the fraudulent practices, who would not have originated them; for the public are aware of the low prices fallaciously produced by the frauds, but do not find out at first, if ever, that the article is not worth the lower price, and they will not go on paying a higher price for a better article, and the honest dealer is placed at a terrible disadvantage. Thus the frauds, begun by a few, become customs of the trade, and the morality of the trading classes is more and more deteriorated.

On this point, therefore, Socialists have really made out the existence not only of a great evil, but of one which grows and tends to grow with the growth of population and wealth. It must be said, however, that society has never yet used the means which are already in its power of grappling with this evil. The laws against commercial frauds are very defective, and their execution still more so. Laws of this description have no chance of being really enforced unless it is the special duty of some one to enforce them. They are specially in need of a public prosecutor. It is still to be discovered how far it is possible to repress by means of the criminal law a class of misdeeds which are now seldom brought before the tribunals, and to which, when brought, the judicial administration of this country is most unduly lenient. The most important class, however, of these frauds, to the mass of the people, those which affect the price or quality of articles of daily consumption, can be in a great measure overcome by the institution of cooperative stores. By this plan any body of consumers who form themselves into an association for the purpose, are enabled to pass over the retail dealers and obtain their articles direct from the wholesale merchants, or, what is better (now that wholesale cooperative agencies have been established), from the producers, thus freeing themselves from the heavy tax now paid to the distributing classes and at the same time eliminate the usual perpetrators of adulterations and other frauds. Distribution thus becomes a work performed by agents selected and paid by those who have no interest in anything but the cheapness and goodness of the article; and the distributors are capable of being thus reduced to the numbers which the quantity of work to be done really requires. The difficulties of the plan consist in the skill and trustworthiness required in the managers, and the imperfect nature of the control which can be exercised over them by the body at large. The great success and rapid growth of the system prove, however, that these difficulties are, in some tolerable degree, overcome. At all events, if the beneficial tendency of the competition of retailers in promoting cheapness is foregone, and has to be replaced by other securities, the mischievous tendency of the same competition in deteriorating quality is at any rate got rid of; and the prosperity of the cooperative stores shows that this benefit is obtained not only without detriment to cheapness, but with great advantage to it, since the profits of the concerns enable them to return to the consumers a large percentage on the price of every article supplied to them. So far, therefore, as this class of evils is concerned, an effectual remedy is already in operation, which, though suggested by and partly grounded on socialistic principles, is consistent with the existing constitution of property.

With regard to those greater and more conspicuous economical frauds, or malpractices equivalent to frauds, of which so many deplorable cases have become notorious—committed by merchants and bankers between themselves or between them and those who have trusted them with money, such a remedy as above described is not available, and the only resources which the present constitution of society affords against them are a sterner reprobation by opinion, and a more efficient repression by the law. Neither of these remedies has had any approach to an effectual trial. It is on the occurrence of insolvencies that these dishonest practices usually come to light; the perpetrators take their place, not in the class of malefactors, but in that of insolvent debtors; and the laws of this and other countries were formerly so savage against simple insolvency, that by one of those reactions to which the opinions of mankind are liable, insolvents came to be regarded mainly as objects of compassion, and it seemed to be thought that the hand both of law and of public opinion could hardly press too lightly upon them. By an error in a contrary direction to the ordinary one of our law, which in the punishment of offenses in general wholly neglects the question of reparation to the sufferer, our bankruptcy laws have for some time treated the recovery for creditors of what is left of their property as almost the sole object, scarcely any importance being attached to the punishment of the bankrupt for any misconduct which does not directly interfere with that primary purpose. For three or four years past there has been a slight counter-reaction, and more than one bankruptcy act has been passed, somewhat less indulgent to the bankrupt; but the primary object regarded has still been the pecuniary interest of the creditors, and criminality in the bankrupt himself, with the exception of a small number of well-marked offenses, gets off almost with impunity. It may be confidently affirmed, therefore, that, at least in this country, society has not exerted the power it possesses of making mercantile dishonesty dangerous to the perpetrator. On the contrary, it is a gambling trick in which all the advantage is on the side of the trickster: if the trick succeeds it makes his fortune, or preserves it; if it fails, he is at most reduced to poverty, which was perhaps already impending when he determined to run the chance, and he is classed by those who have not looked closely into the matter, and even by many who have, not among the infamous but among the unfortunate. Until a more moral and rational mode of dealing with culpable insolvency has been tried and failed, commercial dishonesty cannot be ranked among evils the prevalence of which is inseparable from commercial competition.

Another point on which there is much misapprehension on the part of Socialists, as well as of Trades Unionists and other partisans of Labor against Capital, relates to the proportions in which the produce of the country is really shared and the amount of what is actually diverted from those who produce it, to enrich other persons. I forbear for the present to speak of the land, which is a subject apart. But with respect to capital employed in business, there is in the popular notions a great deal of illusion. When, for instance, a capitalist invests £20,000 in his business, and he draws from it an income of (suppose) £2,000 a year, the common impression is as if he was the beneficial owner both of the £20,000 and of the £2,000, while the laborers own nothing but their wages. The truth, however, is that he only obtains the £2,000 on condition of applying no part of the £20,000 to his own use. He has the legal control over it, and might squander it if he chose, but if he did he would not have the £2,000 a year also. As long as he derives an income from his capital he has not the option of withholding it from the use of others. As much of his invested capital as consists of buildings, machinery, and other instruments of production, are applied to production and are not applicable to the support or enjoyment of any one. What is so applicable (including what is laid out in keeping up or renewing the buildings and instruments) is paid away to laborers, forming their remuneration and their share in the division of the produce. For all personal purposes they have the capital and he has but the profits, which it only yields to him on condition that the capital itself is employed in satisfying not his own wants, but those of laborers. The proportion which the profits of capital usually bear to the capital itself (or rather to the circulating portion of it) is the ratio which the capitalist's share of the produce bears to the aggregate share of the laborers. Even of his own share a small part only belongs to him as the owner of capital. The portion of the produce which falls to capital merely as capital is measured by the interest of money, since that is all that the owner of capital obtains when he contributes nothing to production except the capital itself. Now the interest of capital in the public funds, which are considered to be the best security, is at the present prices (which have not varied much for many years) about three and one-third percent. Even in this investment there is some little risk—risk of repudiation, risk of being obliged to sell out at a low price in some commercial crisis.

Estimating these risks at 1/3 percent, the remaining 3 percent may be considered as the remuneration of capital, apart from insurance against loss. On the security of a mortgage 4 percent is generally obtained, but in this transaction there are considerably greater risks—the uncertainty of titles to land under our bad system of law; the chance of having to realize the security at a great cost in law charges; and liability to delay in the receipt of the interest, even when the principal is safe. When mere money independently of exertion yields a larger income, as it sometimes does, for example, by shares in railway or other companies, the surplus is hardly ever an equivalent for the risk of losing the whole, or part, of the capital by mismanagement, as in the case of the Brighton Railway, the dividend of which, after having been 6 percent per annum, sunk to from nothing to 1½ percent, and shares which had been bought at 120 could not be sold for more than about 43. When money is lent at the high rates of interest one occasionally hears of, rates only given by spendthrifts and needy persons, it is because the risk of loss is so great that few who possess money can be induced to lend to them at all. So little reason is there for the outcry against "usury" as one of the grievous burthens of the working classes. Of the profits, therefore, which a manufacturer or other person in business obtains from his capital no more than about 3 percent can be set down to the capital itself. If he were able and willing to give up the whole of this to his laborers, who already share among them the whole of his capital as it is annually reproduced from year to year, the addition of their weekly wages would be inconsiderable. Of what he obtains beyond 3 percent a great part is insurance against the manifold losses he is exposed to, and cannot safely be applied to his own use, but requires to be kept in reserve to cover those losses when they occur. The remainder is properly the remuneration of his skill and industry—the wages of his labor of superintendence. No doubt if he is very successful in business these wages of his are extremely liberal, and quite out of proportion to what the same skill and industry would command if offered for hire. But, on the other hand, he runs a worse risk than that of being out of employment; that of doing the work without earning anything by it, of having the labor and anxiety without the wages. I do not say that the drawbacks balance the privileges, or that he derives no advantage from the position which makes him a capitalist and employer of labor, instead of a skilled superintendent letting out his services to others; but the amount of his advantage must not be estimated by the great prizes alone. If we subtract from the gains of some the losses of others, and deduct from the balance a fair compensation for the anxiety, skill, and labor of both, grounded on the market price of skilled superintendence, what remains will be, no doubt, considerable, but yet, when compared to the entire capital of the country, annually reproduced and dispensed in wages, it is very much smaller than it appears to the popular imagination; and were the whole of it added to the share of the laborers it would make a less addition to that share than would be made by any important invention in machinery, or by the suppression of unnecessary distributors and other "parasites of industry." To complete the estimate, however, of the portion of the produce of industry which goes to remunerate capital we must not stop at the interest earned out of the produce by the capital actually employed in producing it, but must include that which is paid to the former owners of capital which has been unproductively spent and no longer exists, and is paid, of course, out of the produce of other capital. Of this nature is the interest of national debts, which is the cost a nation is burthened with for past difficulties and dangers, or for past folly or profligacy of its rulers, more or less shared by the nation itself. To this must be added the interest on the debts of landowners and other unproductive consumers; except so far as the money borrowed may have been spent in remunerative improvement of the productive powers of the land. As for landed property itself—the appropriation of the rent of land by private individuals—I reserve, as I have said, this question for discussion hereafter; for the tenure of land might be varied in any manner considered desirable, all the land might be declared the property of the State, without interfering with the right of property in anything which is the product of human labor and abstinence.

It seemed desirable to begin the discussion of the Socialist question by these remarks in abatement of Socialist exaggerations, in order that the true issues between Socialism and the existing state of society might be correctly conceived. The present system is not, as many Socialists believe, hurrying us into a state of general indigence and slavery from which only Socialism can save us. The evils and injustices suffered under the present system are great, but they are not increasing; on the contrary, the general tendency is towards their slow diminution. Moreover the inequalities in the distribution of the produce between capital and labor, however they may shock the feeling of natural justice, would not by their mere equalization afford by any means so large a fund for raising the lower levels of remuneration as Socialists, and many besides Socialists, are apt to suppose. There is not any one abuse or injustice now prevailing in society by merely abolishing which the human race would pass out of suffering into happiness. What is incumbent on us is a calm comparison between two different systems of society, with a view of determining which of them affords the greatest resources for overcoming the inevitable difficulties of life. And if we find the answer to this question more difficult, and more dependent upon intellectual and moral conditions, than is usually thought, it is satisfactory to reflect that there is time before us for the question to work itself out on an experimental scale, by actual trial. I believe we shall find that no other test is possible of the practicability or beneficial operation of Socialist arrangements; but that the intellectual and moral grounds of Socialism deserve the most attentive study, as affording in many cases the guiding principles of the improvements necessary to give the present economic system of society its best chance.

Four

The Difficulties of Socialism

Among those who call themselves Socialists, two kinds of persons may be distinguished. There are, in the first place, those whose plans for a new order of society, in which private property and individual competition are to be superseded and other motives to action substituted, are on the scale of a village community or township, and would be applied to an entire country by the multiplication of such self-acting units; of this character are the systems of Owen, of Fourier, and the more thoughtful and philosophic Socialists generally. The other class, who are more a product of the Continent than of Great Britain and may be called the revolutionary Socialists, propose to themselves a much bolder stroke. Their scheme is the management of the whole productive resources of the country by one central authority, the general government. And with this view some of them avow as their purpose that the working classes, or somebody in their behalf, should take possession of all the property of the country, and administer it for the general benefit.

Whatever be the difficulties of the first of these two forms of Socialism, the second must evidently involve the same difficulties and many more. The former, too, has the great advantage that it can be brought into operation progressively, and can prove its capabilities by trial. It can be tried first on a select population and extended to others as their education and cultivation permit. It need not, and in the natural order of things would not, become an engine of subversion until it had shown itself capable of being also a means of reconstruction. It is not so with the other; the aim of that is to substitute the new rule for the old at a single stroke, and to exchange the amount of good realized under the present system, and its large possibilities of improvement, for a plunge without any preparation into the most extreme form of the problem of carrying on the whole round of the operations of social life without the motive power which has always hitherto worked the social machinery. It must be acknowledged that those who would play this game on the strength of their own private opinion, unconfirmed as yet by any experimental verification—who would forcibly deprive all who have now a comfortable physical existence of their only present means of preserving it, and would brave the frightful bloodshed and misery that would ensue if the attempt was resisted—must have a serene confidence in their own wisdom on the one hand and a recklessness of other people's sufferings on the other, which Robespierre and St. Just, hitherto the typical instances of those united attributes, scarcely came up to. Nevertheless this scheme has great elements of popularity which the more cautious and reasonable form of Socialism has not; because what it professes to do it promises to do quickly, and holds out hope to the enthusiastic of seeing the whole of their aspirations realized in their own time and at a blow.

The peculiarities, however, of the revolutionary form of Socialism will be most conveniently examined after the considerations common to both the forms have been duly weighed.

The produce of the world could not attain anything approaching to its present amount, nor support anything approaching to the present number of its inhabitants, except upon two conditions: abundant and costly machinery, buildings, and other instruments of production; and the power of undertaking long operations and waiting a considerable time for their fruits. In other words, there must be a large accumulation of capital, both fixed in the implements and buildings, and circulating, that is, employed in maintaining the laborers and their families during the time which elapses before the productive operations are completed and the products come in. This necessity depends on physical laws, and is inherent in the condition of human life; but these requisites of production, the capital, fixed and circulating, of the country (to which has to be added the land, and all that is contained in it), may either be the collective property of those who use it, or may belong to individuals; and the question is, which of these arrangements is most conducive to human happiness. What is characteristic of Socialism is the joint ownership by all the members of the community of the instruments and means of production; which carries with it the consequence that the division of the produce among the body of owners must be a public act, performed according to rules laid down by the community. Socialism by no means excludes private ownership of articles of consumption; the exclusive right of each to his or her share of the produce when received, either to enjoy, to give, or to exchange it. The land, for example, might be wholly the property of the community for agricultural and other productive purposes, and might be cultivated on their joint account, and yet the dwelling assigned to each individual or family as part of their remuneration might be as exclusively theirs, while they continued to fulfill their share of the common labors, as any one's house now is; and not the dwelling only, but any ornamental ground which the circumstances of the association allowed to be attached to the house for purposes of enjoyment. The distinctive feature of Socialism is not that all things are in common, but that production is only carried on upon the common account, and that the instruments of production are held as common property. The *practicability* then of Socialism, on the scale of Mr. Owen's or M. Fourier's villages, admits of no dispute. The attempt to manage the whole production of a nation by one central organization is a totally different matter; but a mixed agricultural and manufacturing association of from two thousand to four thousand inhabitants under any tolerable circumstances of soil and climate would be easier to manage than many a joint stock company. The question to be considered is, whether this joint management is likely to be as efficient and successful as the managements of private industry by private capital. And this question has to be considered in a double aspect; the efficiency of the directing mind, or minds, and that of the simple workpeople. And in order to state this question in its simplest form, we will suppose the form of Socialism to be simple Communism, *i.e.,* equal division of the produce among all the sharers, or, according to M. Louis Blanc's still higher standard of justice, apportionment of it according to difference of need, but without making any difference of reward according to the nature of the duty nor according to the supposed merits or services of the individual. There are other forms of Socialism, particularly Fourierism, which do, on considerations of justice or expediency, allow differences of remuneration for different kinds or degrees of service to the community; but the consideration of these may be for the present postponed.

The difference between the motive powers in the economy of society under private property and under Communism would be greatest in the case of the directing minds. Under the present system, the direction being entirely in the hands of the person or persons who own (or are personally responsible for) the capital, the whole benefit of the difference between the best administration and the worst under which the business can continue to be carried on accrues to the person or persons who control the administration: they reap the whole profit of good management except so far as their self-interest or liberality induce them to share it with their subordinates; and they suffer the whole detriment of mismanagement except so far as this may cripple their subsequent power of employing labor. This strong personal motive to do their very best and utmost for the efficiency and economy of the operations, would not exist under Communism; as the managers would only receive out of the produce the same equal dividend as the other members of the association. What would remain would be the interest common to all in so managing affairs as to make the dividend as large as possible; the incentives of public spirit, of conscience, and of the honor and credit of the managers. The force of these motives, especially when combined, is great. But it varies greatly in different persons, and is much greater for some purposes than for others. The verdict of experience, in the imperfect degree of moral cultivation which mankind have yet reached, is that the motive of conscience and that of credit and reputation, even when they are of some strength, are, in the majority of cases, much stronger as restraining than as impelling forces—are more to be depended on for preventing wrong, than for calling forth the fullest energies in the pursuit of ordinary occupations. In the case of most men the only inducement which has been found sufficiently constant and unflagging to overcome the ever-present influence of indolence and love of ease, and induce men to apply themselves unrelaxingly to work for the most part in itself dull and unexciting, is the prospect of bettering their own economic condition and that of their family; and the closer the connection of every increase of exertion with a corresponding increase of its fruits, the more powerful is its motive. To suppose the contrary would be to imply that with men as they now are, duty and honor are more powerful principles of action than personal interest, not solely as to special acts and forbearances respecting which those sentiments have been exceptionally cultivated, but in the regulation of their whole lives; which no one, I suppose, will affirm. It may be said that this inferior efficacy of public and social feelings is not inevitable—is the result of imperfect education. This I am quite ready to admit, and also that there are even now many individual exceptions to the general infirmity. But before these exceptions can grow into a majority, or even into a very large minority, much time will be required. The education of human beings is one of the most difficult of all arts, and this is one of the points in which it has hitherto been least successful; moreover improvements in general education are necessarily very gradual, because the future generation is educated by the present, and the imperfections of the teachers set an invincible limit to the degree in which they can train their pupils to be better than themselves. We must therefore expect, unless we are operating upon a select portion of the population, that personal interest will for a long time be a more effective stimulus to the most vigorous and careful conduct of the industrial business of society than motives of a higher character. It will be said that at present the greed of personal gain by its very excess counteracts its own end by the stimulus it gives to reckless and often dishonest risks. This it does, and under Communism that source of evil would generally be absent. It is probable, indeed, that enterprise either of a bad or of a good kind would be a deficient element, and that business in general would fall very much under the dominion of routine; rather, as the performance of duty in such communities has to be enforced by external sanctions, the more nearly each person's duty can be reduced to fixed rules, the easier it is to hold him to its performance. A circumstance which increases the probability of this result is the limited power which the managers would have of independent action. They would of course hold their authority from the choice of the community, by whom their function might at any time be withdrawn from them; and this would make it necessary for them, even if not so required by the constitution of the community, to obtain the general consent of the body before making any change in the established mode of carrying on the concern. The difficulty of persuading a numerous body to make a change in their accustomed mode of working, of which change the trouble is often great, and the risk more obvious to their minds than the advantage, would have a great tendency to keep things in their accustomed track. Against this it has to be set, that choice by the persons who are directly interested in the success of the work, and who have practical knowledge and opportunities of judgment, might be expected on the average to produce managers of greater skill than the chances of birth, which now so often determine who shall be the owner of the capital. This may be true; and though it may be replied that the capitalist by inheritance can also, like the community, appoint a manager more capable than himself, this would only place him on the same level of advantage as the community, not on a higher level. But it must be said on the other side that under the Communist system the persons most qualified for the management would be likely very often to hang back from undertaking it. At present the manager, even if he be a hired servant, has a very much larger remuneration than the other persons concerned in the business; and there are open to his ambition higher social positions to which his function of manager is a stepping-stone. On the Communist system none of these advantages would be possessed by him; he could obtain only the same dividend out of the produce of the community's labor as any other member of it; he would no longer have the chance of raising himself from a receiver of wages into the class of capitalists; and while he could be in no way better off than any other laborer, his responsibilities and anxieties would be so much greater that a large proportion of mankind would be likely to prefer the less onerous position. This difficulty was foreseen by Plato as an objection to the system proposed in his Republic of community of goods among a governing class; and the motive on which he relied for inducing the fit persons to take on themselves, in the absence of all the ordinary inducements, the cares and labors of government, was the fear of being governed by worse men. This, in truth, is the motive which would have to be in the main depended upon; the persons most competent to the management would be prompted to undertake the office to prevent it from falling into less competent hands. And the motive would probably be effectual at times when there was an impression that by incompetent management the affairs of the community were going to ruin, or even only decidedly deteriorating. But this motive could not, as a rule, expect to be called into action by the less stringent inducement of merely promoting improvement; unless in the case of inventors or schemers eager to try some device from which they hoped for great and immediate fruits; and persons of this kind are very often unfitted by over-sanguine temper and imperfect judgment for the general conduct of affairs, while even when fitted for it they are precisely the kind of persons against whom the average man is apt to entertain a prejudice, and they would often be unable to overcome the preliminary difficulty of persuading the community both to adopt their project and to accept them as managers. Communistic management would thus be, in all probability, less favorable than private management to that striking out of new paths and making immediate sacrifices for distant and uncertain advantages, which, though seldom unattended with risk, is generally indispensable to great improvements in the economic condition of mankind, and even to keeping up the existing state in the face of a continual increase of the number of mouths to be fed.

We have thus far taken account only of the operation of motives upon the managing minds of the association. Let us now consider how the case stands in regard to the ordinary workers.

These, under Communism, would have no interest, except their share of the general interest, in doing their work honestly and energetically. But in this respect matters would be no worse than they now are in regard to the great majority of the producing classes. These, being paid by fixed wages, are so far from having any direct interest of their own in the efficiency of their work, that they have not even that share in the general interest which every worker would have in the Communistic organization. Accordingly, the inefficiency of hired labor, the imperfect manner in which it calls forth the real capabilities of the laborers, is matter of common remark. It is true that a character for being a good workman is far from being without its value, as it tends to give him a preference in employment, and sometimes obtains for him higher wages. There are also possibilities of rising to the position of foreman, or other subordinate administrative posts, which are not only more highly paid than ordinary labor, but sometimes open the way to ulterior advantages. But on the other side is to be set that under Communism the general sentiment of the community, composed of the comrades under whose eyes each person works, would be sure to be in favor of good and hard working, and unfavorable to laziness, carelessness, and waste. In the present system not only is this not the case, but the public opinion of the workman class often acts in the very opposite direction: the rules of some trade societies actually forbid their members to exceed a certain standard of efficiency, lest they should diminish the number of laborers required for the work; and for the same reason they often violently resist contrivances for economizing labor. The change from this to a state in which every person would have an interest in rendering every other person as industrious, skillful, and careful as possible (which would be the case under Communism), would be a change very much for the better.

It is, however, to be considered that the principal defects of the present system in respect to the efficiency of labor may be corrected, and the chief advantages of Communism in that respect may be obtained, by arrangements compatible with private property and individual competition. Considerable improvement is already obtained by piece-work, in the kinds of labor which admit of it. By this the workman's personal interest is closely connected with the quantity of work he turns out—not so much with its quality, the security for which still has to depend on the employer's vigilance; neither does piece-work carry with it the public opinion of the workman class, which is often, on the contrary, strongly opposed to it, as a means of (as they think) diminishing the market for laborers. And there is really good ground for their dislike of piece-work, if, as is alleged, it is a frequent practice of employers, after using piece-work to ascertain the utmost which a good workman can do, to fix the price of piece-work so low that by doing that utmost he is not able to earn more than they would be obliged to give him as day wages for ordinary work.

But there is a far more complete remedy than piece-work for the disadvantages of hired labor, viz. what is now called industrial partnership—the admission of the whole body of laborers to a participation in the profits, by distributing among all who share in the work, in the form of a percentage on their earnings, the whole or a fixed portion of the gains after a certain remuneration has been allowed to the capitalist. This plan has been found of admirable efficacy, both in this country and abroad. It has enlisted the sentiments of the workmen employed on the side of the most careful regard by all of them to the general interest of the concern; and by its joint effect in promoting zealous exertion and checking waste, it has very materially increased the remuneration of every description of labor in the concerns in which it has been adopted. It is evident that this system admits of indefinite extension and of an indefinite increase in the share of profits assigned to the laborers, short of that which would leave to the managers less than the needful degree of personal interest in the success of the concern. It is even likely that when such arrangements become common, many of these concerns would at some period or another, on the death or retirement of the chiefs, pass, by arrangement, into the state of purely cooperative associations.

It thus appears that as far as concerns the motives of exertion in the general body, Communism has no advantage which may not be reached under private property, while as respects the managing heads it is at a considerable disadvantage. It has also some disadvantages which seem to be inherent in it, through the necessity under which it lies of deciding in a more or less arbitrary manner questions which, on the present system, decide themselves, often badly enough, but spontaneously.

It is a simple rule, and under certain aspects a just one, to give equal payment to all who share in the work. But this is a very imperfect justice unless the work also is apportioned equally. Now the many different kinds of work required in every society are very unequal in hardness and unpleasantness. To measure these against one another, so as to make quality equivalent to quantity, is so difficult that Communists generally propose that all should work by turns at every kind of labor. But this involves an almost complete sacrifice of the economic advantages of the division of employments, advantages which are indeed frequently overestimated (or rather the counter-considerations are underestimated) by political economists, but which are nevertheless, in the point of view of the productiveness of labor, very considerable, for the double reason that the cooperation of employment enables the work to distribute itself with some regard to the special capacities and qualifications of the worker, and also that every worker acquires greater skill and rapidity in one kind of work by confining himself to it. The arrangement, therefore, which is deemed indispensable to a just distribution would probably be a very considerable disadvantage in respect of production. But further, it is still a very imperfect standard of justice to demand the same amount of work from every one. People have unequal capacities of work, both mental and bodily, and what is a light task for one is an insupportable burthen to another. It is necessary, therefore, that there should be a dispensing power, an authority competent to grant exemptions from the ordinary amount of work, and to proportion tasks in some measure to capabilities. As long as there are any lazy or selfish persons who like better to be worked for by others than to work, there will be frequent attempts to obtain exemptions by favor or fraud, and the frustration of these attempts will be an affair of considerable difficulty, and will by no means be always successful. These inconveniences would be little felt, for some time at least, in communities composed of select persons, earnestly desirous of the success of the experiment; but plans for the regeneration of society must consider average human beings, and not only them but the large residuum of persons greatly below the average in the personal and social virtues. The squabbles and ill-blood which could not fail to be engendered by the distribution of work whenever such persons have to be dealt with, would be a great abatement from the harmony and unanimity which Communists hope would be found among the members of their association. That concord would, even in the most fortunate circumstances, be much more liable to disturbance than Communists suppose. The institution provides that there shall be no quarrelling about material interests; individualism is excluded from that department of affairs. But there are other departments from which no institutions can exclude it: there will still be rivalry for reputation and for personal power. When selfish ambition is excluded from the field in which, with most men, it chiefly exercises itself, that of riches and pecuniary interest, it would betake itself with greater intensity to the domain still open to it, and we may expect that the struggles for preeminence and for influence in the management would be of great bitterness when the personal passions, diverted from their ordinary channel, are driven to seek their principal gratification in that other direction. For these various reasons it is probable that a Communist association would frequently fail to exhibit the attractive picture of mutual love and unity of will and feeling which we are often told by Communists to expect, but would often be torn by dissension and not unfrequently broken up by it.

Other and numerous sources of discord are inherent in the necessity which the Communist principle involves, of deciding by the general voice questions of the utmost importance to every one, which on the present system can be and are left to individuals to decide, each for his own case. As an example, take the subject of education. All Socialists are strongly impressed with the all-importance of the training given to the young, not only for the reasons which apply universally, but because their demands being much greater than those of any other system upon the intelligence and morality of the individual citizen, they have even more at stake than any other societies on the excellence of their educational arrangements. Now under Communism these arrangements would have to be made for every citizen by the collective body, since individual parents, supposing them to prefer some other mode of educating their children, would have no private means of paying for it, and would be limited to what they could do by their own personal teaching and influence. But every adult member of the body would have an equal voice in determining the collective system designed for the benefit of all. Here, then, is a most fruitful source of discord in every association. All who had any opinion or preference as to the education they would desire for their own children, would have to rely for their chance of obtaining it upon the influence they could exercise in the joint decision of the community.

It is needless to specify a number of other important questions affecting the mode of employing the productive resources of the association, the conditions of social life, the relations of the body with other associations, &c., on which difference of opinion, often irreconcilable, would be likely to arise. But even the dissensions which might be expected would be a far less evil to the prospects of humanity than a delusive unanimity produced by the prostration of all individual opinions and wishes before the decree of the majority. The obstacles to human progression are always great, and require a concurrence of favorable circumstances to overcome them; but an indispensable condition of their being overcome is, that human nature should have freedom to expand spontaneously in various directions, both in thought and practice; that people should both think for themselves and try experiments for themselves, and should not resign into the hands of rulers, whether acting in the name of a few or of the majority, the business of thinking for them, and of prescribing how they shall act. But in Communist associations private life would be brought in a most unexampled degree within the dominion of public authority, and there would be less scope for the development of individual character and individual preferences than has hitherto existed among the full citizens of any state belonging to the progressive branches of the human family. Already in all societies the compression of individuality by the majority is a great and growing evil; it would probably be much greater under Communism, except so far as it might be in the power of individuals to set bounds to it by selecting to belong to a community of persons like-minded with themselves.

From these various considerations I do not seek to draw any inference against the possibility that Communistic production is capable of being at some future time the form of society best adapted to the wants and circumstances of mankind. I think that this is, and will long be, an open question, upon which fresh light will continually be obtained, both by trial of the Communistic principle under favorable circumstances, and by the improvements which will be gradually effected in the working of the existing system, that of private ownership. The one certainty is, that Communism, to be successful, requires a high standard of both moral and intellectual education in all the members of the community—moral, to qualify them for doing their part honestly and energetically in the labor of life under no inducement but their share in the general interest of the association, and their feelings of duty and sympathy towards it; intellectual, to make them capable of estimating distant interests and entering into complex considerations, sufficiently at least to be able to discriminate, in these matters, good counsel from bad. Now I reject altogether the notion that it is impossible for education and cultivation such as is implied in these things to be made the inheritance of every person in the nation; but I am convinced that it is very difficult, and that the passage to it from our present condition can only be slow. I admit the plea that in the points of moral education on which the success of Communism depends, the present state of society is demoralizing, and that only a Communistic association can effectually train mankind for Communism. It is for Communism, then, to prove, by practical experiment, its power of giving this training. Experiments alone can show whether there is as yet in any portion of the population a sufficiently high level of moral cultivation to make Communism succeed, and to give to the next generation among themselves the education necessary to keep up that high level permanently. If Communist associations show that they can be durable and prosperous, they will multiply, and will probably be adopted by successive portions of the population of the more advanced countries as they become morally fitted for that mode of life. But to force unprepared populations into Communist societies, even if a political revolution gave the power to make such an attempt, would end in disappointment.

If practical trial is necessary to test the capabilities of Communism, it is no less required for those other forms of Socialism which recognize the difficulties of Communism and contrive means to surmount them. The principal of these is Fourierism, a system which, if only as a specimen of intellectual ingenuity, is highly worthy of the attention of any student, either of society or of the human mind. There is scarcely an objection or a difficulty which Fourier did not foresee, and against which he did not make provision beforehand by self-acting contrivances, grounded, however, upon a less high principle of distributive justice than that of Communism, since he admits inequalities of distribution and individual ownership of capital, but not the arbitrary disposal of it. The great problem which he grapples with is how to make labor attractive, since, if this could be done, the principal difficulty of Socialism would be overcome. He maintains that no kind of useful labor is necessarily or universally repugnant, unless either excessive in amount or devoid of the stimulus of companionship and emulation, or regarded by mankind with contempt. The workers in a Fourierist village are to class themselves spontaneously in groups, each group undertaking a different kind of work, and the same person may be a member not only of one group but of any number; a certain minimum having first been set apart for the subsistence of every member of the community, whether capable or not of labor, the society divides the remainder of the produce among the different groups, in such shares as it finds attract to each the amount of labor required, and no more; if there is too great a run upon particular groups it is a sign that those groups are over-remunerated relatively to others; if any are neglected their remuneration must be made higher. The share of produce assigned to each group is divided in fixed proportions among three elements—labor, capital, and talent; the part assigned to talent being rewarded by the suffrages of the group itself, and it is hoped that among the variety of human capacities all, or nearly all, will be qualified to excel in some group or other. The remuneration for capital is to be such as is found sufficient to induce savings from individual consumption, in order to increase the common stock to such point as is desired. The number and ingenuity of the contrivances for meeting minor difficulties, and getting rid of minor inconveniences, is very remarkable. By means of these various provisions it is the expectation of Fourierists that the personal inducements to exertion for the public interest, instead of being taken away, would be made much greater than at present, since every increase of the service rendered would be much more certain of leading to increase of reward than it is now, when accidents of position have so much influence. The efficiency of labor, they therefore expect, would be unexampled, while the saving of labor would be prodigious, by diverting to useful occupations that which is now wasted on things useless or hurtful, and by dispensing with the vast number of superfluous distributors, the buying and selling for the whole community being managed by a single agency. The free choice of individuals as to their manner of life would be no further interfered with than would be necessary for gaining the full advantages of cooperation in the industrial operations. Altogether, the picture of a Fourierist community is both attractive in itself and requires less from common humanity than any other known system of Socialism; and it is much to be desired that the scheme should have that fair trial which alone can test the workableness of any new scheme of social life.[1]

The result of our review of the various difficulties of Socialism has led us to the conclusion that the various schemes for managing the productive resources of the country by public instead of private agency have a case for a trial, and some of them may eventually establish their claims to preference over the existing order of things, but that they are at present workable only by the *élite* of mankind, and have yet to prove their power of training mankind at large to the state of improvement which they presuppose. Far more, of course, may this be said of the more ambitious plan which aims at taking possession of the whole land and capital of the country, and beginning at once to administer it on the public account. Apart from all consideration of injustice to the present possessors, the very idea of conducting the whole industry of a country by direction from a single center is so obviously chimerical, that nobody ventures to propose any mode in which it should be done; and it can hardly be doubted that if the revolutionary Socialists attained their immediate object, and actually had the whole property of the country at their disposal, they would find no other practicable mode of exercising their power over it than that of dividing it into portions, each to be made over to the administration of a small Socialist community. The problem of management, which we have seen to be so difficult even to a select population well prepared beforehand, would be thrown down to be solved as best it could by aggregations united only by locality, or taken indiscriminately from the population, including all the malefactors, all the idlest and most vicious, the most incapable of steady industry, forethought, or self-control, and a majority who, though not equally degraded, are yet, in the opinion of Socialists themselves, as far as regards the qualities essential for the success of Socialism, profoundly demoralized by the existing state of society. It is saying but little to say that the introduction of Socialism under such conditions could have no effect but disastrous failure, and its apostles could have only the consolation that the order of society as it now exists would have perished first, and all who benefit by it would be involved in the common ruin—a consolation which to some of them would probably be real, for if appearances can be trusted the animating principle of too many of the revolutionary Socialists is hate; a very excusable hatred of existing evils, which would vent itself by putting an end to the present system at all costs even to those who suffer by it, in the hope that out of chaos would arise a better Kosmos, and in the impatience of desperation respecting any more gradual improvement. They are unaware that chaos is the very most unfavorable position for setting out in the construction of a Kosmos, and that many ages of conflict, violence, and tyrannical oppression of the weak by the strong must intervene; they know not that they would plunge mankind into the state of nature so forcibly described by Hobbes *(Leviathan,* Part I. ch. xiii.), where every man is an enemy to every man:

> In such condition there is no place for industry, because the fruit thereof is uncertain, and consequently no culture of the earth, no navigation, no use of the commodities that may be imported by sea, no commodious building, no instruments of moving and removing such things as require such force, no knowledge of the face of the earth, no account of time, no arts, no letters, no society; and, which is worst of all, continual fear and danger of violent death; and the life of man solitary, poor, nasty, brutish, and short.

If the poorest and most wretched members of a so-called civilized society are in as bad a condition as every one would be in that worst form of barbarism produced by the dissolution of civilized life, it does not follow that the way to raise them would be to reduce all others to the same miserable state. On the contrary, it is by the aid of the first who have risen that so many others have escaped from the general lot, and it is only by better organization of the same process that it may be hoped in time to succeed in raising the remainder.

NOTE

1. The principles of Fourierism are clearly set forth and powerfully defended in the various writings of M. Victor Considérant, especially that entitled *La Destinée Sociale;* but the curious inquirer will do well to study them in the writings of Fourier himself; where he will find unmistakable proofs of genius, mixed, however, with the wildest and most unscientific fancies respecting the physical world, and much interesting but rash speculation on the past and future history of humanity. It is proper to add that on some important social questions, for instance on marriage, Fourier had peculiar opinions, which, however, as he himself declares, are quite independent of, and separable from, the principles of his industrial system.

Five

The Idea of Private Property not Fixed but Variable

The preceding considerations appear sufficient to show that an entire renovation of the social fabric, such as is contemplated by Socialism, establishing the economic constitution of society upon an entirely new basis, other than that of private property and competition, however valuable as an ideal, and even as a prophecy of ultimate possibilities, is not available as a present resource, since it requires from those who are to carry on the new order of things qualities both moral and intellectual, which require to be tested in all, and to be created in most; and this cannot be done by an Act of

Parliament, but must be, on the most favorable supposition, a work of considerable time. For a long period to come the principle of individual property will be in possession of the field; and even if in any country a popular movement were to place Socialists at the head of a revolutionary government, in however many ways they might violate private property, the institution itself would survive, and would either be accepted by them or brought back by their expulsion, for the plain reason that people will not lose their hold of what is at present their sole reliance for subsistence and security until a substitute for it has been got into working order. Even those, if any, who had shared among themselves what was the property of others would desire to keep what they had acquired, and to give back to property in the new hands the sacredness which they had not recognized in the old.

But though, for these reasons, individual property has presumably a long term before it, if only of provisional existence, we are not, therefore, to conclude that it must exist during that whole term unmodified, or that all the rights now regarded as appertaining to property belong to it inherently, and must endure while it endures. On the contrary, it is both the duty and the interest of those who derive the most direct benefit from the laws of property to give impartial consideration to all proposals for rendering those laws in any way less onerous to the majority. This, which would in any case be an obligation of justice, is an injunction of prudence also, in order to place themselves in the right against the attempts which are sure to be frequent to bring the Socialist forms of society prematurely into operation.

One of the mistakes oftenest committed, and which are the sources of the greatest practical errors in human affairs, is that of supposing that the same name always stands for the same aggregation of ideas. No word has been the subject of more of this kind of misunderstanding than the word property. It denotes in every state of society the largest powers of exclusive control over things (and sometimes, unfortunately, over persons) which the law accords, or which custom, in that state of society, recognizes; but these powers of exclusive use and control are very various, and differ greatly in different countries and in different states of society.

For instance, in early states of society, the right of property did not include the right of bequest. The power of disposing of property by will was in most countries of Europe a rather late institution; and long after it was introduced it continued to be limited in favor of what were called natural heirs. Where bequest is not permitted, individual property is only a life interest. And in fact, as has been so well and fully set forth by Sir Henry Maine in his most instructive work on Ancient Law, the primitive idea of property was that it belonged to the family, not the individual. The head of the family had the management and was the person who really exercised the proprietary rights. As in other respects, so in this, he governed the family with nearly despotic power. But he was not free so to exercise his power as to defeat the co-proprietors of the other portions; he could not so dispose of the property as to deprive them of the joint enjoyment or of the succession. By the laws and customs of some nations the property could not be alienated without the consent of the male children; in other cases the child could by law demand a division of the property and the assignment to him of his share, as in the story of the Prodigal Son. If the association kept together after the death of the head, some other member of it, not always his son, but often the eldest of the family, the strongest, or the one selected by the rest, succeeded to the management and to the managing rights, all the others retaining theirs as before. If, on the other hand, the body broke up into separate families, each of these took away with it a part of the property. I say the property, not the inheritance, because the process was a mere continuance of existing rights, not a creation of new; the manager's share alone lapsed to the association.

Then, again, in regard to proprietary rights over immovables (the principal kind of property in a rude age) these rights were of very varying extent and duration. By the Jewish law property in immovables was only a temporary concession; on the Sabbatical year it returned to the common stock to be redistributed; though we may surmise that in the historical times of the Jewish state this rule may have been successfully evaded. In many countries of Asia, before European ideas intervened, nothing existed to which the expression property in land, as we understand the phrase, is strictly applicable. The ownership was broken up among several distinct parties, whose rights were determined rather by custom than by law. The government was part owner, having the right to a heavy rent. Ancient ideas and even ancient laws limited the government share to some particular fraction of the gross produce, but practically there was no fixed limit. The government might make over its share to an individual, who then became possessed of the right of collection and all the other rights of the state, but not those of any private person connected with the soil. These private rights were of various kinds. The actual cultivators, or such of them as had been long settled on the land, had a right to retain possession; it was held unlawful to evict them while they paid the rent—a rent not in general fixed by agreement, but by the custom of the neighborhood. Between the actual cultivators and the state, or the substitute to whom the state had transferred its rights, there were intermediate persons with rights of various extent. There were officers of government who collected the state's share of the produce, sometimes for large districts, who, though bound to pay over to government all they collected, after deducting a percentage, were often hereditary officers. There were also, in many cases, village communities, consisting of the reputed descendants of the first settlers of a village, who shared among themselves either the land or its produce according to rules established by custom, either cultivating it themselves or employing others to cultivate it for them, and whose rights in the land approached nearer to those of a landed proprietor, as understood in England, than those of any other party concerned. But the proprietary right of the village was not individual, but collective; inalienable (the rights of individual sharers could only be sold or mortgaged with the consent of the community) and governed by fixed rules. In medieval Europe almost all land was held from the sovereign on tenure of service, either military or agricultural; and in Great Britain even now, when the services as well as all the reserved rights of the sovereign have long since fallen into disuse or been commuted for taxation, the theory of the law does not acknowledge an absolute right of property in land in any individual; the fullest landed proprietor known to the law, the freeholder, is but a "tenant" of the Crown. In Russia, even when the cultivators of the soil were serfs of the landed proprietor, his proprietary right in the land was limited by rights of theirs belonging to them as a collective body managing its own affairs, and with which he could not interfere. And in most of the countries of continental Europe when serfage was abolished or went out of use, those who had cultivated the land as serfs remained in possession of rights as well as subject to obligations. The great land reforms of Stein and his successors in Prussia consisted in abolishing both the rights and the obligations, and dividing the land bodily between the proprietor and the peasant, instead of leaving each of them with a limited right over the whole. In other cases, as in Tuscany, the *metayer* farmer is virtually co-proprietor with the landlord, since custom, though not law, guarantees to him a permanent possession and half the gross produce, so long as he fulfills the customary conditions of his tenure.

Again, if rights of property over the same things are of different extent in different countries, so also are they exercised over different things. In all countries at a former time, and in some countries still, the right of property extended and extends to the ownership of human beings. There has often been property in public trusts, as in judicial offices, and a vast multitude of others in France before the Revolution; there are still a few patent offices in Great Britain, though I believe they will cease by operation of law on the death of the present holders; and we are only now abolishing property in army rank. Public bodies, constituted and endowed for public purposes, still claim the same inviolable right of property in their estates which individuals have in theirs, and though a sound political morality does not acknowledge this claim, the law supports it. We thus see that the right of property is differently interpreted, and held to be of different extent, in different times and places; that the conception entertained of it is a varying conception, has been frequently revised, and may admit of still further revision. It is also to be noticed that the revisions which it has hitherto undergone in the progress of society have generally been improvements. When, therefore, it is maintained, rightly or wrongly, that some change or modification in the powers exercised over things by the persons legally recognized as their proprietors would be beneficial to the public and conducive to the general improvement, it is no good answer to this merely to say that the proposed change conflicts with the idea of property. The idea of property is not some one thing, identical throughout history and incapable of alteration, but is variable like all other creations of the human mind; at any given time it is a brief expression denoting the rights over things conferred by the law or custom of some given society at that time; but neither on this point nor on any other has the law and custom of a given time and place a claim to be stereotyped for ever. A proposed reform in laws or customs is not necessarily objectionable because its adoption would imply, not the adaptation of all human affairs to the existing idea of property, but the adaptation of existing ideas of property to the growth and improvement of human affairs. This is said without prejudice to the equitable claim of proprietors to be compensated by the state for such legal rights of a proprietary nature as they may be dispossessed of for the public advantage. That equitable claim, the grounds and the just limits of it, are a subject by itself, and as such will be discussed hereafter. Under this condition, however, society is fully entitled to abrogate or alter any particular right of property which on sufficient consideration it judges to stand in the way of the public good. And assuredly the terrible case which, as we saw in a former chapter, Socialists are able to make out against the present economic order of society, demands a full consideration of all means by which the institution may have a chance of being made to work in a manner more beneficial to that large portion of society which at present enjoys the least share of its direct benefits.

GREAT BOOKS IN PHILOSOPHY PAPERBACK SERIES

ETHICS

Aristotle—*The Nicomachean Ethics*	$8.95
Marcus Aurelius—*Meditations*	5.95
Jeremy Bentham—*The Principles of Morals and Legislation*	8.95
John Dewey—*The Moral Writings of John Dewey, Revised Edition* (edited by James Gouinlock)	10.95
Epictetus—*Enchiridion*	3.95
Immanuel Kant—*Fundamental Principles of the Metaphysic of Morals*	4.95
John Stuart Mill—*Utilitarianism*	4.95
George Edward Moore—*Principia Ethica*	8.95
Friedrich Nietzsche—*Beyond Good and Evil*	8.95
Bertrand Russell—*Bertrand Russell On Ethics, Sex, and Marriage* (edited by Al Seckel)	18.95
Benedict de Spinoza—*Ethics* and *The Improvement of the Understanding*	9.95

SOCIAL AND POLITICAL PHILOSOPHY

Aristotle—*The Politics*	7.95
Mikhail Bakunin—*The Basic Bakunin: Writings, 1869–1871* (translated and edited by Robert M. Cutler)	10.95
Edmund Burke—*Reflections on the Revolution in France*	7.95
John Dewey—*Freedom and Culture*	10.95
G. W. F. Hegel—*The Philosophy of History*	9.95
Thomas Hobbes—*The Leviathan*	7.95
Sidney Hook—*Paradoxes of Freedom*	9.95
Sidney Hook—*Reason, Social Myths, and Democracy*	11.95
John Locke—*Second Treatise on Civil Government*	4.95
Niccolo Machiavelli—*The Prince*	4.95
Karl Marx/Frederick Engels—*The Economic and Philosophic Manuscripts of 1844* and *The Communist Manifesto*	6.95
John Stuart Mill—*Considerations on Representative Government*	6.95
John Stuart Mill—*On Liberty*	4.95
John Stuart Mill—*On Socialism*	7.95
John Stuart Mill—*The Subjection of Women*	4.95
Friedrich Nietzsche—*Thus Spake Zarathustra*	9.95

Thomas Paine—*Rights of Man* 7.95
Plato—*Plato on Homosexuality: Lysis, Phaedrus,* and *Symposium* 6.95
Plato—*The Republic* 9.95
Jean-Jacques Rousseau—*The Social Contract* 5.95
Mary Wollstonecraft—*A Vindication of the Rights of Women* 6.95

METAPHYSICS/EPISTEMOLOGY

Aristotle—*De Anima* 6.95
Aristotle—*The Metaphysics* 9.95
George Berkeley—*Three Dialogues Between Hylas and Philonous* 4.95
René Descartes—*Discourse on Method* and *The Meditations* 6.95
John Dewey—*How We Think* 10.95
Epicurus—*The Essential Epicurus: Letters, Principal Doctrines, Vatican Sayings, and Fragments* (translated, and with an introduction, by Eugene O'Connor) 5.95
Sidney Hook—*The Quest for Being* 11.95
David Hume—*An Enquiry Concerning Human Understanding* 4.95
David Hume—*Treatise of Human Nature* 9.95
William James—*Pragmatism* 7.95
Immanuel Kant—*Critique of Pure Reason* 9.95
Gottfried Wilhelm Leibniz—*Discourse on Method* and the *Monadology* 6.95
Plato—*The Euthyphro, Apology, Crito,* and *Phaedo* 5.95
Bertrand Russell—*The Problems of Philosophy* 8.95
Sextus Empiricus—*Outlines of Pyrrhonism* 8.95

PHILOSOPHY OF RELIGION

Ludwig Feuerbach—*The Essence of Christianity* 8.95
David Hume—*Dialogues Concerning Natural Religion* 5.95
John Locke—*A Letter Concerning Toleration* 4.95
Thomas Paine—*The Age of Reason* 13.95
Bertrand Russell—*Bertrand Russell On God and Religion* (edited by Al Seckel) 18.95

ESTHETICS

Aristotle—*The Poetics* 5.95